Southern Living® GARDEN GUIDE

Lawns & Ground Covers

Series Editor: Lois Trigg Chaplin

Text by Barbara Pleasant

OXMOOR HOUSE®

Contents

Southern Living® is a federally registered trademark of Southern Living, Inc.

Library of Congress Catalog Number: 96-71088
ISBN: 0-8487-2248-5
Manufactured in the United States of America
First Printing 1997

We're Here for You!
We at Oxmoor House are dedicated to serving you with reliable information that expands your imagination and enriches your life. We welcome your comments and suggestions. Please write us at:

Oxmoor House, Inc.
Editor, LAWNS & GROUND COVERS Garden Guide
2100 Lakeshore Drive
Birmingham, AL 35209

Editor-in-Chief: Nancy Fitzpatrick Wyatt
Editorial Director, Special Interest Publications:
Ann H. Harvey
Senior Editor, Editorial Services: Olivia Kindig Wells
Art Director: James Boone

Southern Living Garden Guide
LAWNS & GROUND COVERS

Series Editor: Lois Trigg Chaplin
Assistant Editor: Kelly Hooper Troiano
Copy Editor: Jacqueline B. Giovanelli
Editorial Assistant: Allison D. Ingram
Garden Editor, *Southern Living*: Linda C. Askey
Indexer: Katharine R. Wiencke
Concept Designer: Eleanor Cameron
Designer: Carol Loria
Illustrator: Melanie Magee
Senior Photographer, *Southern Living*: Van Chaplin
Production and Distribution Director: Phillip Lee
Associate Production Manager: Vanessa C. Richardson
Production Assistant: Faye Porter Bonner

Our appreciation to the staff of *Southern Living* magazine for their contributions to this book.

Liriope

Cover: *Tall fescue lawn bordered by liriope*
Frontispiece: *St. Augustine lawn edged with liriope and Japanese ardisia*

Centipede (left) and Bermuda grasses

Lawns and Ground Covers Primer

The first impression of your home is often influenced by your creative use of lawns and ground covers.

When thoughtfully placed, lawns and ground covers bring color and texture to your garden's floor in much the same way that rugs provide color and texture inside a house. A well-conditioned lawn helps you satisfy both functional and aesthetic needs, serving as a comfortable surface for outdoor activities while bringing a restful unity to the landscape. Ground covers, which are plants other than grass that blanket the ground, allow you to add beautiful details to background areas and emphasize the flow of the landscape's design.

Growing a healthy lawn requires work and patience. But if you don't enjoy lawn care, you'll be glad to know that today's trend in landscaping is toward smaller lawns and lower-maintenance ground covers. Compared to lawns, most ground covers need less care and are often easier to grow. They are ideal for tight spots, slippery slopes, and places that are too shady for grass. However, no ground cover is tough enough to stand up to a game of touch football or even an outdoor dinner party. For this reason, you may want at least a small area of lawn.

You can enjoy both the play space of a toe-tingling lawn and the low maintenance of ground covers by using grass and ground covers to carpet your landscape. To help you make the most of what these plants have to offer, this book includes a section on designing with lawns and ground covers as well as useful information on how to grow warm- and cool-season lawn grasses and popular ground covers.

Magical things happen when you cultivate your garden's floor. The velvety texture of grass flatters anything growing nearby, and ground covers can turn trouble spots into lovely tapestries of green. Both lawns and ground covers can make your yard more beautiful, comfortable, and enjoyable.

The proper combination of lawn grass and ground cover can create a ruglike lawn.

Designing Your Landscape

A carpet of grass and ground cover sets the stage for the rest of the landscape.

Landscapes are best thought of as a series of outdoor rooms, each with its own particular purpose. In the front yard, choose simple designs that flatter your house. Give special attention to ways that make the entry feel like a spacious and inviting outdoor foyer. If you often use your backyard for recreation and entertaining, set personal comfort and privacy as top priorities. Consider transforming side yards into cozy passageways or screened utility areas.

The ways in which you use the various portions of your landscape strongly influence the type of lawn and ground cover that you will need in each area. When designing with lawns and ground covers, your goal should always be to furnish the garden's floor with plants that will make each space more functional, attractive, and easy to maintain. Choosing the best plants—from fine-textured lawn grasses to larger-leafed ground covers—requires careful analysis of your site, your family's needs, and the look you want to achieve.

This planting of mondo grass helps direct visitors up the walkway to the front door.

Assessing Your Landscape

The first step in developing an effective lawn design is to learn as much as possible about your site. Your decisions about where to locate lawn areas or swaths of ground covers will be affected by sunlight, existing trees, the lay of the land, the size and style of your house, and the planned uses of the space. Identify problem areas such as low spots where grass won't grow or steep slopes that are impossible to mow. Think about how you can design your landscape so that it looks attractive from the street as well as from the most frequently used rooms in your house. The more you know about your site, the fewer mistakes you will make when choosing the plants that will serve as living carpets.

A strategically placed lawn can provide a space for play as well as an area for entertaining.

Determining Proper Sun and Shade

Light is an important consideration when it comes to designing your garden's floor. Grass provides a fine, luxurious texture in the garden, and it likes sun, ideally eight hours or more. Good light helps grass grow into a strong, tightly knit turf that naturally resists weeds. When you try to grow a sun-loving grass such as Bermuda in a mixture of sun and shade, it will be thin and weedy where the shade falls. This may look fine in the summer, when both weeds and grass are green, but in winter you will be left with a patchwork pattern of green cool-season weeds surrounded by the dormant Bermuda's sea of light tan.

You can grow a healthy lawn in light shade if you choose grasses that are the most tolerant of shade, such as tall fescue in the upper South and St. Augustine in the lower South. However, if the primary sources of shade are the shadows from your house or large

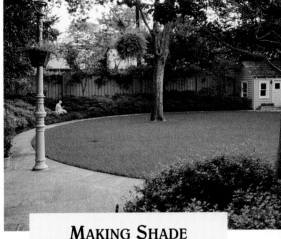

High limbs of tall shade trees allow some sunlight to reach lawn grasses growing beneath them.

trees, design a smaller lawn that fits the sunniest spot and use shade-tolerant ground covers in the areas too shady for grass. Expand paved surfaces, such as walkways and patios, to make your landscape easy to use and maintain in sun or shade.

Working around Trees

It is preferable to design a lawn that will not require you to mow around a lot of tree trunks. This means that you must find an alternative to grass. Shrub borders or large ground cover plantings placed around the trees are an easy solution.

Try expanding a planting of ground cover so that it becomes a broad evergreen island under scattered trees. This will tie the trees together visually and reduce the total size of the lawn. Used this way, ground covers also help unify the entire landscape.

Competition for light, nutrients, and water seriously stresses even the most shade-tolerant grass growing beneath trees. This is less of a problem for ground covers, which can be mulched lightly to help retain soil moisture and generally require less fertilizer than lawn grasses. Ground covers are an easy way to cover areas under trees where grass struggles to survive.

MAKING SHADE LIGHTER

Many plants that grow well in shade do best with what is called **high shade**—shade from high tree limbs rather than low ones. Shade-tolerant grasses also like high shade because they get more light. One way to encourage the success of a lawn under trees is to lighten the shade by removing the lower limbs of large trees to at least 10 feet from the ground.

Masses of shade-tolerant holly ferns and azaleas link trees visually while saving you the work of maintaining grass under trees.

7

A ground cover of liriope helps prevent erosion on this slope.

Taming Slopes and Trouble Spots

In studying your lot, you may discover flat places with drainage problems or slopes that are subject to erosion. In general, grasses need good drainage and a very slight slope, or grade, to allow storm water to run off. Most grasses will not grow well where the ground remains soggy for long periods.

If you have heavy clay soil, a flat lot, or an area where water collects from nearby rooftops or paved surfaces, you may need to install an underground drainage system or create a surface drainage path (or *swale*) to channel the water away. If drainage is a serious problem, you will need to consult a landscape architect or an engineer.

On the other hand, excessively sloping land drains well but may be difficult to mow. Often the solution is to simply cover the slope with plants that require little attention. Steep slopes may need the physical reinforcement of a retaining wall, but slopes that rise less than 2 feet vertically for every 4 feet of length (**Diagram A**), or rise at less than a 45-degree angle, can be planted with ground covers that develop extensive roots, such as English ivy or periwinkle. Shrubbier ground covers, such as cotoneaster, creeping juniper, or wintercreeper, make good slope stabilizers as well.

You can also grow some types of grass on gentle slopes. Bermuda, Zoysia, and other creeping grasses that knit themselves together into a tight turf are best. But because mowing a slope can be dangerously slippery, use grass only where the slope rises less than 1 foot vertically for every 4 feet of length (**Diagram B**). Also plan to establish turf on slopes using good-quality sod (rather than seeds or sprigs), for properly installed sod will fight erosion from the day it is planted.

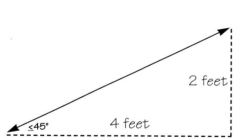

Diagram A:
Maximum slope for ground covers

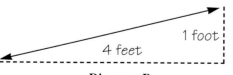

Diagram B:
Maximum slope for grass

Designing for Outdoor Living

After you've taken into account site factors such as sun, shade, drainage, and slope, study the way you and your family will use your yard. Areas that will be used for play or entertaining have different requirements than those that are seldom used yet often seen. If low maintenance is a priority, think about limiting the space given to lawn. Most ground covers require less upkeep once established, allowing you to spend more time enjoying your yard and less time maintaining it.

A Place To Play

Grass makes an excellent playing surface, so you will probably need a larger lawn if you have children. However, the areas beneath swing sets and other play equipment receive more wear than grass

A grassy lawn that serves as a playground will need extra care to keep it green and thick.

can handle. Covering the ground beneath play equipment with cushioning mulch will keep the surface from turning into bare mud.

If you entertain regularly, locate lawn areas adjacent to your terrace or deck to provide overflow space for guests. Even if you seldom entertain, consider including a small lawn near the showiest parts of your landscape. It will give you a place to relax and enjoy the view, and the fine texture of the turf will serve as flattering contrast for the flowers, shrubs, trees, or stonework that may accent your yard.

Passageways

No grass or ground cover will grow well where people and pets continually walk, compacting the ground and wearing out the plants. These areas call for paths. Depending on the design, you can choose from a permanent walkway made of brick, concrete, or stone or an informal path of pine straw, mulch, or pebbles held in place with a hard edging.

Stepping-stones work well in narrow corridors subject to light foot traffic. If you use stepping-stones within a carpet of plants, make sure you select plants, such as dwarf mondo grass, that don't grow too high. In a lawn, set the stepping-stones down into the soil about ½ inch lower than the mowing height of your grass, or nearly level with the soil's surface. You will be able to mow the area more easily by running the mower over the stones. Within a ground cover planting, you may need to occasionally trim back the plants to form neat edges.

Accentuate the edges of any walkway by outlining it with a ground cover planted in a broader border. Bear in mind that a long, continuous line of a single plant will make the walkway seem longer.

One design trick that gives passageways a definite feel of direction and purpose is to flank them with a border that broadens as it nears an entryway or a gate to another garden room. You can easily achieve this funnel effect with a single ground cover or a combination of ground covers and low-growing shrubs.

Designing with Lawns

A careful analysis of nearly any landscape reveals places that will support a good lawn and others where ground covers will do a better job. Don't worry that a small lawn might detract from the overall appeal of your landscape. Just as an area rug gives a cozy feeling to the interior of a home, a modest-sized planting of smooth grass serves as a welcome mat for the rest of the garden. A small lawn defines

To create an easily maintained path, use a combination of pavers and ground cover, such as mondo grass.

space, adds a focal point, and provides color and texture. And it is easier to take care of a small, well-defined lawn than one that sprawls across your yard and merges into the yard next door.

In the backyard, the same lawn you design as a play surface can link your patio or deck to distant areas that are special rooms themselves, such as a natural woodland, a water garden, a wildflower area, or a perennial border. A small but distinctive lawn also can act as a unifying element in the garden. For example, if most of your yard space is taken up with a gazebo, herb garden, or other features that you enjoy, a small, centrally located lawn area offers welcome simplicity and makes the backyard feel less cluttered.

Shaping Your Lawn

The shape of a lawn is most important. A rectangular plot implies order and organization and complements a formal garden. Circular or semicircular shapes also have a special place; because a circular lawn has no specific direction, it can tie together unrelated parts of the landscape. The best shape for your lawn may be determined by the way the house is situated on the lot. When the house and lot are square to the street, a rectangular shape fits in easily, but a rectangular lawn would look forced into place in a pie-shaped lot. For this type of lot, a circular lawn will be more pleasing.

The rectangular shape of this lawn contributes to the landscape's formal look.

11

LAWN DESIGN TIPS

• Realize your limitations. It is much better to have a small, handsome lawn than a large, poorly kept one. If your time is limited, a small lawn may be all you can manage.

• Shape the lawn to suit your garden. Geometric shapes look formal, while free-form lines are casual.

• Have shrub and ground cover beds encompass tree trunks to simplify lawn maintenance.

• Choose spreading shrubs or ground covers for slopes to reduce erosion and make maintenance easier.

• Make sure that you can reach lawn areas with a mower and that all areas are large enough to maneuver in easily. Narrow strips, wavy borders, or tight corners can be awkward to mow.

One pitfall to beware of is **wiggles,** or irregularly shaped lawns with several curving edges. Keep in mind that the best curves for the edges of a lawn are broad arcs, like the lines you might get if you cut a perfect circle into sections. Too many curves can make the lawn difficult to mow along the edges and look disheveled, even when the grass is freshly mowed and the edges are trimmed. It is fine to follow the natural contours of your lot when designing your lawn, but always keep the curves as uncomplicated as possible.

Pay special attention to the line formed by the front edge of a lawn—the one you see first when approaching the house. If this line doesn't please the eye, neither will the lawn. Because front yards are

The lawn's curved edges make broad arcs that contrast nicely with the straight edge along the driveway.

often bordered by straight-edged streets, driveways, or sidewalks, it is usually safest to retain a straight line. Or you may choose to introduce a regular form, such as a circle, for the high-visibility edge. Save random curves for less prominent edges or for more informal spaces in other parts of your yard. Above all, strive for a simple shape that flows easily from one area to another without a lot of wiggles.

Framing Your Lawn

To make the most of a small lawn or accentuate the beauty of a larger one, you should add a frame. For small lawns, an edging of stone or perhaps a brick mowing strip works well as a visual frame. In places where the edges of the lawn fade into shade or your neighbor's property, use broad borders of evergreen ground cover plants to define the shape of the lawn and provide beautiful textural contrast. That contrast can be especially arresting in winter. Consider, for example, the bright green winter color of an overseeded lawn framed by bronze-green English ivy: the green grass nearly leaps out at the viewer. A golden Zoysia grass lawn in the same spot is visually quieter but no less attractive.

Good-quality turf requires too much maintenance to be grown just to fill up empty space. If you have a large yard and all that space is covered in grass, you'll spend a great deal of time mowing it. Unless you really enjoy lawn care, consider redesigning your yard so that the lawn you have is the lawn you need. The rest of your garden can be planted with ground covers or well-designed shrub and flower borders.

A brick edging provides a frame for this lawn as well as a border for flowerbeds.

A small circular lawn turns a shapely tree into a focal point while attractive brickwork gives the lawn a neat, manicured look.

CREATIVE DESIGNS FOR LAWNS

These pages offer a few examples of lawn designs that are important components of the overall landscape plan as well as being easy to maintain.

This lawn serves as overflow space for outdoor entertaining and makes a pleasing view from the rear rooms of the house.

If you have a spacious lot bordered by shrubs and trees, use a lawn as a broad passageway.

Narrow swaths of lawn provide a relaxing green band and textural contrast between a brick patio and the complexity of a perennial border.

Sometimes ground cover can replace a lawn entirely.

Designing with Ground Covers

Any area of your yard that you don't need for outdoor activities or for a garden bed for vegetables, herbs, or flowers is a candidate for a carefully chosen ground cover. Many of the same ideas that apply to designing lawns apply to designing ground cover plantings as well, particularly the use of lines. Orderly straight lines impart a formal feel, while curves convey a more casual mood.

Evergreen ground covers are often used to accentuate lines in the landscape because their colors and textures contrast vividly with lawns and with larger shrubs and trees. For example, a border planting of liriope or ivy used to line a walkway or enclose a small lawn boldly frames the shape of each element.

This very boldness of evergreen ground covers makes them useful in adding order and unity to the landscape. In formal situations where you want a high degree of symmetry, matching swaths of ground cover on each side of the yard can help create the perfect balance that formal designs require. This balanced use of ground covers is popular in small city yards, where beds of naturally neat ground covers such as common periwinkle, Japanese star jasmine, or mondo grass can be used on either side of the front walkway. In a front yard

This ground cover of English ivy ties together trees and, at the same time, gives strong definition to the lawn.

with sufficient paved walkways to handle all foot traffic, ground covers can take the place of the front lawn altogether. Frame these high-visibility plantings with a low wall or a decorative fence to make them look neat and manicured.

Ground Cover Combinations

Where ground covers are used to fill shade, stabilize steep slopes, or solve other site problems in a small area, one or two plant types are best for a neater, more uniform look. If you want more excitement than a solid swath of ground cover provides, add stones for textural contrast or use a few taller shrubs or small trees to introduce vertical interest.

In a large landscape, you may set out more than one type of ground cover, especially if the ground covers you use have different textures and are planted in large masses. For example, grasslike liriope or mondo grass used to blanket a shady slope can be complemented by an adjacent broad-leafed ground cover, such as ajuga or pachysandra. Or you might frame a planting of ferns with a low creeping ground cover, such as periwinkle. Keep your eyes open for plant combinations that work well in your area, and repeat those combinations to achieve balance and unity within your design. To visually link your ground cover plantings with the rest of a small garden, repeat the ground cover in a container.

Two design tricks are often used with ground covers. One is to use repetitive plantings of the same ground cover in different parts of your yard to unify the landscape. The other trick is to stretch vertical or horizontal swaths of a ground cover on either side of a driveway or walkway, so that the planting appears to have existed before the hard surface was laid down.

Ivy, liriope, and mondo grass form a true low-maintenance landscape. The short, fine-textured mondo grass creates the illusion of grass on both sides of the entry but doesn't require frequent mowing.

Bright ground covers such as this variegated liriope bring permanent color contrast to a garden.

Colorful Ground Covers

Ground covers can bring much-needed color to the garden, another consideration when designing with these plants. The simplest color combination—green and white—plays out beautifully in Silver Edge pachysandra, Variegata ajuga, or various ivies with white-edged leaves. If you mix types of variegated plants, you may create a fussy look, but a refined mass of a single variegated foliage brings contrast to dark shade.

Ground cover plants with neutral tones, particularly those with gray-green foliage such as lamb's-ears, can help play down conflicts of hue between colorful plants. At the same time, they can highlight the subtle tones of attractive stonework. Some ground cover plants can also serve to fill off-season color gaps in low-maintenance landscapes. Cotoneaster, for example, produces jewel-like fall berries, while selections of wintercreeper turn burgundy red with the onset of winter.

Carpets in Bloom

Several ground covers produce colorful flowers, which can be enjoyed by themselves or in combination with other blooming plants. Ground covers that trail and tangle along the ground, including Japanese star jasmine and periwinkles, have seasonal blooms. These plants and all the ivies can also be underplanted with small daffodils or jonquils for more color in early spring. Spider lilies work well grown beneath many ground covers and bloom in late summer to early fall when brightly colored flowers are often in short supply.

A caution about underplanting bulbs in ground covers: Use only those bulbs that are likely to bloom well for many years, and keep the selection of colors and species as simple as you can. Daffodils, Spanish bluebells, and spider lilies are three dependable choices. Once a ground cover planting is well established, the last thing you want to do is dig it up to replace bulbs.

A slope covered with ajuga becomes a mass of colorful flowers in spring.

Besides adding beauty, this run of stones serves as a swale to direct excess water while toning down the setting's wild look. The network of Southern shield ferns helps to stabilize the slope.

LANDSCAPING SPECIAL SITES WITH GROUND COVERS

Ground covers can contribute to the overall look of a garden and in some cases also remedy a landscape problem. The different ground covers shown in these photographs work well for the specific design that incorporates them.

A bench on a small wood deck within a lush planting of pachysandra is a delightful refuge in this lowland garden.

Ground covers planted in a rhythmic pattern along a broad walkway make the entry to the house inviting and easy to maintain.

In keeping with the primitive beauty of this damp, shaded backyard, wild mosses provide dramatically different ground cover. Shade-tolerant perennial hostas occupy the high ground, while a ribbon of rock helps drain the most flood-prone areas.

Getting Started with Lawn Grasses

Like ornamental plants, lawn grasses vary in their adaptability to locales and growing conditions. Matching a grass to your site is essential to success.

Whether you are planting a new lawn, renovating an old one, or just patching a few bare spots, the type of grass you choose can make or break the project. Turf specialists divide lawn grasses into two groups: warm-season grasses, such as Bahia, Bermuda, buffalo grass, centipede, St. Augustine, and Zoysia, and cool-season grasses, such as Kentucky bluegrass, perennial ryegrass, and tall fescue. Warm-season grasses grow rapidly in hot weather and go dormant after a frost. Cool-season grasses behave just the opposite. They become vibrantly green and lush in fall and spring but have trouble surviving the hot summer sun in the lower and coastal South.

The individual profiles of lawn grasses that begin on page 55 will help you choose the best grass for your yard. You will also need to think about several other factors. Is the lawn to be located in sun or shade? Will it be walked on often or will it serve primarily as a visual foreground for your home? How much lawn maintenance are you willing to do? The answers to these questions will help you select the most suitable grass and steer you toward the best way to establish a new lawn or renovate an old one.

This Zoysia lawn flourishes in the spring and summer and turns a golden brown during the winter.

RECOMMENDED GRASSES FOR THE SOUTH

Grass Name	Type	Hardiness	Texture	Shade Tolerance	Drought Tolerance	Maintenance	Method of Establishment
Bahia	Warm season	Lower South Coastal South	Coarse	Poor	Very good	High	Seed, sod
Bermuda, Hybrid	Warm season	Middle South Lower South Coastal South	Fine	Poor	Good	High	Sod, plugs
Buffalo Grass	Warm season	Upper South Middle South	Fine	Poor	Very good	Very low	Seed, sod, or plugs
Centipede	Warm season	Lower South Coastal South	Coarse	Poor	Fair	Low	Sod, plugs, or seed
Fescue, Tall	Cool season	Upper South Middle South	Medium	Good	Good	Moderate	Seed, sod
Kentucky Bluegrass	Cool season	Upper South Middle South	Fine	Fair	Poor	Moderate	Seed, sod
Perennial Ryegrass	Cool season	Upper South Middle South	Medium	Poor	Poor	Moderate	Seed
St. Augustine	Warm season	Lower South Coastal South	Coarse	Poor to good, depends on selection	Good	Moderate	Sod, plugs
Zoysia	Warm season	Upper South Middle South	Fine to medium	Fair	Good	Moderate	Sod, plugs

BUYING SOD

Shop carefully when selecting sod. Certified sod is guaranteed to be free of weeds and pests and is worth the cost. Buy the freshest sod available, and plant it as quickly as possible. By working with a local landscape professional, you can probably arrange to have freshly harvested sod delivered exactly when you need it. Water the prepared soil the night before planting to be sure that the ground is moist.

Sod creates an instant lawn.

Selecting Seed or Sod

The two most popular ways to start a lawn are from seed and from *sod* (sheets of mature turf). If you're working with a grass that spreads quickly, you can also plant small chunks of sod called ***plugs***. (See page 29 for more information about plugs.) Every planting method has its merits and drawbacks, but a few grasses, such as Zoysia and hybrids of Bermuda and St. Augustine, can't be planted from seed.

Seeding. Sowing seeds is the least expensive way to start a new lawn. Compared to using sod, seeding is a bargain if you are planting Bahia, tall fescue, or a cool-season mixture of perennial ryegrass, tall fescue, and other cool-season grasses. Seven pounds of tall fescue seed can cover 1,000 square feet of lawn and costs less than $20; a bale of wheat straw to mulch the seeded ground costs around $3.50.

A seeded lawn appears green in about three weeks but takes several months to grow into wear-resistant turf. (It takes centipede two years.) If the site slopes enough to make water erosion a problem, the seed may wash away, and the grass may not grow fast enough to hold the prepared soil in place. In this case, consider using the same grass in sod form for planting the parts of the site that slope. This will take some advance planning and phone calls to local sources to be sure that your selection of grass is available as both seed and sod.

Sodding. Regardless of the site, sod gives you an instant lawn that will have fewer problems with weeds as it becomes established. The greatest drawbacks with sod are its cost and its limited planting season. Price varies with the type of grass but generally ranges between $3 and $8 per square yard.

The best time to plant sod is at the beginning of its growing season, that is, midspring to early summer for warm-season grasses and early fall for cool-season grasses. You have probably seen warm-season grasses such as Bermuda and Zoysia being planted from sod in commercial landscapes in the fall, but this is a risky practice. Warm-season sod that doesn't have a chance to develop good roots before it becomes dormant may be injured by the cold and is easily invaded by winter weeds. It is much safer to plant these grasses from sod in spring or early summer, when they will have several months to establish roots before winter.

Getting Ready To Plant

The first step in establishing a healthy lawn is to prepare the soil properly before planting. Kill existing grasses and weeds by spraying with a nonselective weedkiller, such as Roundup or Finale. Read the label before buying the product to be sure it is recommended for areas that you plan to plant soon. After the unwanted vegetation dies, till the area to break up dead grass and compacted soil. When you till, work in a 1- to 2-inch layer of organic matter, as well as lime if a soil test indicates any is needed. (See page 32 for more information on soil testing.) If you are sowing seeds, apply a high-phosphorus starter fertilizer at this time.

Use a steel garden rake to level the ground and collect chunks of dead grass and stones. If all the old grass didn't come up with the first tilling, till and rake the soil again. Remember, you are establishing a finished grade, so include any slope needed for drainage. If your soil is poor, you may want to top the prepared soil with 2 to 3 inches of topsoil and rake it smooth.

Before you plant, till the ground to break up existing vegetation and loosen the soil.

After tilling, use a steel rake to level the ground and collect any stones or chunks of dead grass that remain in the soil.

A good watering or a gentle rain will help settle the loose soil, but this can take time. The best idea is to go over the area with a *roller,* which is a specialized tool that looks like a barrel with long handles. You can rent a roller at most rental equipment centers. You'll need to fill it with water to make it heavy, but a half-filled barrel is heavy enough to firm the soil without compacting it. Rolling the soil helps reveal sunken areas that you should fill and level before planting. Shave off high areas with a spade. If you're planting Bermuda or Zoysia, which can be mowed lower than other grasses, take particular care to eliminate every small bump or sunken spot in the prepared site.

Be ready to plant shortly after preparing the soil, as a heavy rain can undo a lot of your hard work. If for some unexpected reason you are unable to plant immediately, scatter wheat straw or pine straw over the site until you can barely see the soil through the straw. Don't use hay; it may contain weed seeds. Rake up the straw before you plant your lawn.

A roller helps you identify sunken spots that should be filled before planting.

Starting a Lawn from Seed

Sow grass seed when it is most likely to grow fast and strong. You should plant cool-season grass in early fall (in the South) or early spring (in the North) and warm-season grass in midspring. For best results, follow the seeding rates (pounds of seed per 1,000 square feet) recommended on the seed package. See the adjoining box for a general guideline.

Buying Good Seed

Always begin with high-quality, certified seed. If you can't decide between named selections, ask the dealer. One selection may be better adapted for your site than another, or you may get the best results from a seed mixture or blend. For example, tall fescue seed may be mixed with small amounts of perennial ryegrass for a fast green-up of your yard, or blended with Kentucky bluegrass, which knits with the tall fescue to make a stronger turf. Warm-season grasses that can be grown from seed usually are not blended or mixed

SEEDING RATES

Pounds of Seed
per 1,000 Square Feet

Bahia: 5 to 10
Centipede: 1 to 1½
Fescue, Tall: 5 to 10
Perennial Ryegrass: 5 to 10

with other types of grass seed. When buying any grass seed, check the label for the following: name(s) of selection(s), weed-seed content, germination percentage, and date tested. Inexpensive seed that is old or weedy is not a bargain. Seed should be 99 percent to 99.9 percent weed free and contain no noxious weeds. The label will state that it contains no noxious weeds, as in most states it is illegal to sell seed contaminated with weeds that are noxious in that state.

Seeding Evenly

Seed must be scattered evenly and spaced uniformly for a good stand of grass. Sow seeds using a drop spreader or a hand-cranked seeder; broadcasting seeds by hand will produce a spotty lawn. If you're using a seed mixture or blend, stir the seeds with your hand as you fill the seeder, and try to mix seeds from the top of the bag with seeds from the bottom. To ensure even coverage, sow half the seed while you walk over the area in one direction and the other half of the seed while walking at a right angle to the first direction.

To be sure the seeds are in good contact with the soil, roll the area with a half-filled roller or rake it lightly to partially bury the seeds. Then cover the bed with a sprinkling of weed-free wheat straw to help protect the seeds from drying and washing away. Don't remove the straw when the seed germinates; the straw will rot in place.

At first, water daily with a gentle but soaking sprinkle. Once the grass is 1 to 2 inches tall, water every two or three days. Begin mowing when the grass is 4 inches tall, and fertilize lightly after the third mowing. Allow one full growing season to pass before applying a weedkiller.

Reseeding

Because tall fescue grass grows in tufts, and individual plants don't spread by runners that knit together along the ground, tall fescue lawns benefit from periodic reseeding to keep them growing lush and tight. You may find that in spots that receive more sun in winter than in summer, it is helpful to reseed with a mixture of tall fescue and perennial ryegrass in the fall. The new grass holds the soil firmly despite winter rains and gives excellent winter color. If thin areas are present in early spring, they are best reseeded early in the season.

Use a drop spreader to space grass seed evenly throughout the planting area, thus avoiding a spotty lawn.

A hand-cranked seeder makes it easy to distribute grass seed over a large area.

Overseeding

If you enjoy your warm-season lawn in summer but don't like its tan color in winter, you can overseed it with a type of ryegrass in the fall for a bright green color in winter. One type of inexpensive seed is annual ryegrass. It grows well in light shade but it needs frequent mowing during the winter. In full sun, perennial ryegrass is a better choice if you don't want to mow too much in winter because it doesn't grow as quickly as annual ryegrass. It is important that the perennial grass you use to overseed dies as soon as the weather gets warm so that it doesn't compete with the permanent warm-season grass.

If you overseed a lawn in fall, mow it to a height of about 1 inch or as low as possible without injuring the ***crowns,*** the points at the base of the grass where the blades originate. After this close mowing, rake the lawn clean.

Using a hand-cranked seeder or a broadcast spreader that will scatter seed evenly, sow about 10 pounds of ryegrass seed per 1,000 square feet. Don't sow the seed by hand or it will end up in clumps. Rake the area again lightly to help the seeds settle through the grass so that they come into contact with the soil. If rain is not in the forecast, water the seeded area daily until the new grass seedlings appear.

An overseeded lawn will be a bright, fresh green from fall through early spring.

Planting Sod

Begin by laying the sod on a straight side of the lawn, such as at the edge of the street or driveway. If there are no straight edges, simply divide the area into quadrants with stakes and string, and start by laying the sod on either side of the strings. Never stretch pieces of sod; recruit a helper, if necessary, to move the sheets of sod without breaking them. Lay each rectangular strip of sod as tightly against the adjacent strip as possible without overlapping. Stagger the joints between strips as you would stagger bricks when building a wall. This creates a smooth turf and protects the edges from drying. Filling the joints with sand also helps keep the edges of the sod pieces damp and encourages them to grow together quickly.

To sod a slope, lay the long side of each strip across the face of the slope. As you reach irregular areas, fit the pieces by cutting the sod with a sharp knife or a spade. Set leftover pieces of sod in the shade while you plant the rest of the lawn. After all the sod is in place, press it down with a water-filled roller to make sure the roots are pushed into the soil.

Water the sod daily for the first two weeks, and then every other day, gradually decreasing the frequency of watering to just once a week. When the grass begins to grow, mow and fertilize it as you would an established lawn.

Planting Plugs

Although seeding and sodding are by far the most common methods of establishing a lawn, they are not your only alternatives. Gardeners who are long on patience and short on cash may want to plug grasses that spread. Plugs are small chunks of sod or transplantlike pieces of grass. Grasses that may be started with plugs are Bermuda, centipede, St. Augustine, and Zoysia. Begin by preparing the site the same way you would for planting seed or sod. Time the planting so that you set out plugs in late spring, the beginning of the most active season of growth for these grasses.

To plant plugs, purchase them in trays or make your own using a sharp knife to cut a 3-inch-square plug from a piece of sod. Plugs that are ready-grown in flats can be lifted out of their cells like flower transplants. In a prepared bed, make a hole large enough to accommodate the plug, and place a teaspoon of slow-release starter fertilizer into the hole. Set the plug so the grass is at ground level. Space plugs 1 foot apart. (At this spacing, you will need 7 square

Freshly laid sod will look like carpet tiles until the edges of the sod blocks grow together.

Fill the joints between blocks of sod with sand to keep the sod moist and encourage growth.

PATCH REPAIRS

When lawn problems are very localized or when the lawn has been damaged, you can simply patch the bare areas. To replace thin or damaged turf, clear the area up to the healthy grass. Then use a turning fork to loosen the soil. If the soil is heavy clay or sand, add organic matter to improve soil structure. Rake to the desired grade. Cut sod to fit the bare area, or sow seed, depending on your choice of grass. Care for the newly planted areas as you would a new lawn, keeping them moist during the first critical weeks.

When patching damaged areas of turf, work the soil in that spot before planting.

Blocks of sod laid to repair a lawn will eventually knit with the existing lawn, but you must water them daily during the first few weeks until their roots become established.

yards of sod to cut into plugs to cover 1,000 square feet.) Keep the plugs moist for the first couple of weeks. Thereafter, you may decrease watering as the roots become established. Plugs should form a nice lawn in one to two seasons. Be prepared to pull or spray weeds that are sure to sprout in the bare areas.

Planting Sprigs

Sprigs are 4- to 8-inch long runners of grass that can be planted as you would a cutting. Although sprigs are sometimes mentioned as a way to establish Bermuda, centipede, and St. Augustine grasses, you will find it much easier to plant sod, seed, or plugs. Sprigging is generally done by machine for large commercial plantings.

If you wish to plant sprigs, you will have to make your own because they have no shelf life and are rarely sold. Try collecting shoots that are cut off when you or a neighbor edges a walkway, driveway, or a shrub bed. Prepare 3-inch-deep trenches, fill these halfway with loose soil, and set the sprigs 1 to 1½ inches deep. You can also use a screwdriver to make holes in the soil. Insert the end of the sprig into the hole, and step on the soil to firm it.

Although plugs have a better chance of surviving, sprigs may actually cover an area more quickly. Regular mowing once they are well rooted encourages them to spread. Weed the planted area by hand the first season, and consider overseeding the site with perennial ryegrass during the first winter. This temporary winter lawn grass will go a long way toward discouraging winter weeds while your new lawn fills in.

Caring for Your Lawn

A green lawn makes a garden more beautiful. It is an ideal setting for warm-weather picnics, campouts, and garden parties. With proper care, your lawn can survive all these activities and more. And you won't need to spend every weekend working on it to keep it looking good. But you do need to understand what your lawn requires and then be willing to do the right things at the right time. Each maintenance factor influences the other. For example, too much fertilizer means more mowing. Mowing too low increases how often you'll need to water and how many weeds you'll have.

Guidelines for all major lawn care tasks are discussed on the pages that follow, but these are only guidelines—you have to strike the right balance. Depending on your soil, site, and climate, your lawn may need more or less care than average to keep it in top condition.

Lawns that receive proper care are naturally beautiful and seldom develop serious problems.

With a little knowledge, care, and commitment, you can keep your lawn green and healthy.

ALWAYS DO A SOIL TEST

Before fertilizing your lawn, it pays to check your soil's chemistry. Is the soil acidity (pH) too high or low? How much nitrogen, phosphorus, and potassium does the soil need? In certain areas of the country, salt levels are high; in others, the native soil may be deficient in a crucial element. A soil test will tell you what your soil requires.

Soil test kits are available through your county Agricultural Extension Service office. The kit contains directions for testing, and a form for garden information. Most states charge a small fee, but it is worth the cost to determine exactly what your soil needs to yield beautiful, healthy plants.

Fertilize your lawn at the proper rate to make the most of the growing season.

Fertilizing

A properly fertilized lawn competes with weeds and better withstands attack by insects or diseases. The right fertilizers applied at the right times will also help your lawn survive extreme cold or heat and green-up quickly at the beginning of the growing season. Different grasses have varying fertilizer requirements and schedules depending on the site and soil.

Choosing a Fertilizer

When buying a good lawn fertilizer, choose one that has at least 25 to 30 percent nitrogen in controlled-release form; 50 percent is even better. Look on the label for the words "slow release," "timed release," or "controlled release." A controlled-release fertilizer will be more expensive than those that are not. However, the extra cost is worth it, for you are paying for the slow release of nitrogen over a period of several weeks. This means that the fertilizer will not rush an excessive amount of nitrogen to the soil only to have it leach away before it can provide essential nutrients.

A preferred controlled-release fertilizer contains nitrogen, phosphorus, potassium, and other trace elements such as iron. Nitrogen, referred to by the first number on the fertilizer label, is the element

that will stimulate new foliage, which is why you need to apply it early in the growth cycle. Ammonium nitrate, ammonium sulfate, or urea are sources of nitrogen that break down too quickly; what is not taken up by the grass soon after application is washed away. Also, too much nitrogen released all at one time can seriously burn the lawn.

The second number on the label refers to phosphorus, which encourages rooting and is essential for overall plant health. *Starter fertilizers*, which contain a high percentage of phosphorus, encourage good rooting. However, too much phosphorus in the soil blocks a plant's ability to absorb other nutrients. Because suburban areas that were once agricultural may be high in phosphorus, it is wise to do a soil test before choosing a lawn fertilizer.

Potassium, also called potash on fertilizer labels, is essential to plant metabolism. It is crucial to a plant's cell wall structure as well as its ability to manufacture food. Potassium content, represented by the third number, is often the largest number on winterizer fertilizers, as the additional potassium is thought to encourage tolerance of cold.

The easiest approach to buying fertilizer is to select a name brand controlled-release fertilizer formulated for your type of grass, as there are many variants of fertilizer for specific grass types. For example, centipede grass, which doesn't like too much nitrogen or phosphorus, is best fertilized once a year with a formula that is low in nitrogen and contains no phosphorus. The Lawn Grass Profiles that begin on page 55 include suggestions for specific fertilizers for each grass.

Apply the fertilizer at the rate recommended on the label. Do not overapply. Too much fertilizer can encourage diseases, especially on cool-season grasses in the summer. Overfertilizing will make the lawn grow faster, too, which will mean more mowing.

Fertilizing on Time

Grass needs the most fertilizer during its growing season. For the majority of warm-season grasses, the rule of thumb is to fertilize in spring, summer, and fall. Bahia and centipede are the exceptions, as they actually decline if overfed. Fertilize them just once a year, in spring. With all warm-season grasses, make the spring application after the grass turns green.

Fall fertilization helps a lawn store food for next spring and makes it more tolerant of extreme cold in winter—especially if you didn't fertilize in summer. For this feeding, the key is to use a

THE FERTILIZER LABEL

By law, all fertilizers must carry a label stating the percentage of nutrients they contain. The three numbers always represent the percentage of nitrogen (N), phosphorus (P), and potassium (K). If the package is labeled 16-4-8, it contains 16 percent nitrogen, 4 percent phosphorus, and 8 percent potassium. These are the nutrients most required by a plant, so the combination of nitrogen, phosphorus, and potassium makes up what is called a *complete fertilizer.*

Caring for Your Lawn

Lawns need fertilizer during the growing season to develop into a thick lush turf.

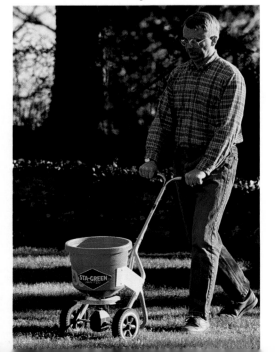

A broadcast spreader helps scatter the fertilizer evenly over the lawn so that each area receives an equal amount.

fertilizer that is low in nitrogen and high in potassium, such as 8-8-25 (often labeled *winterizer*). In most of the South, the best time to apply is in late August or early September, while the lawn is still bright green.

Cool-season grasses require fertilizing in fall, winter, and early spring. Usually one application at the beginning of each season is enough. For example, you can apply a regular lawn fertilizer in September, a winterizer in November, and regular fertilizer again in March.

Spreading Fertilizer

Use a spreader to distribute fertilizer evenly over the lawn. If you just throw the material out by hand, you will end up with green spots and streaks. Choose from three basic tools used to apply lawn fertilizer: drop spreaders, broadcast spreaders, and hose-end sprayers.

A drop spreader is most accurate, but it is also slowest because it drops a swath only as wide as the hopper of the spreader. Drop spreaders are ideal if your lawn is small or if you are applying a fertilizer/weedkiller combination near shrubs and flowerbeds. Many weedkillers are safe for lawns but not for flowers and shrubs, and a drop spreader applies these chemicals only where they need to go.

For lawns 5,000 square feet or larger, you will probably want a broadcast spreader for routine fertilizing. It scatters the material with a whirling action, throwing it in a swath at least 6 feet wide. The width of the swath is adjustable to 10 feet or more on most types of broadcast spreaders, so for large lawns this saves you time and footsteps.

Hose-end sprayers are useful for applying liquid fertilizer for quick green-up, but they can't distribute controlled-release fertilizers. However, several products are available in ready-to-use, hose-end spray bottles that include both lawn fertilizer and chemicals to control weeds. These can be great time-savers, especially if your lawn is small and you want to apply a liquid fertilizer for fast greening.

Using Weedkillers

You may want to use commercial weedkillers to control the crabgrass, dandelion, henbit, and other weeds that are a common problem in lawns. Weedkillers can be divided into two types—pre-emergence weedkillers and post-emergence weedkillers. Pre-emergence weedkillers are usually applied in spring and fall to kill weeds as their seeds sprout. Products labeled as crabgrass preventers or weed preventers are pre-emergence herbicides. Timing is everything with these products; if you spread them after the seeds sprout, they won't do a bit of good. Some pre-emergence weedkillers are combined with granular fertilizers because both of these work best just before the growing season begins, when weeds are sprouting and the lawn is ready to begin new growth.

Post-emergence weedkillers are applied to weeds after they sprout. They are most commonly used for broadleaf weeds, such as dandelion. The best time to apply post-emergence herbicides is when the weeds are young and growing and the lawn has been green for a few weeks. Although generally safe when handled exactly according to label directions, post-emergence herbicides run a higher risk of damaging the lawn. Use them only when weeds are present, and check the label to make sure the product is safe to use on your type of grass.

To reduce existing weeds in a lawn, you might apply a pre-emergence weedkiller in late winter, a post-emergence weedkiller in late spring or early summer (provided weeds are still present), and a pre-emergence weedkiller again in late summer. After a year of such intense weed management, a well-maintained lawn should be weed free on its own. Just be careful not to mow the grass too low. Cutting the lawn too low makes it easy for weed seeds to sprout. (See page 122 for more information about specific weeds.)

(See page 122 for more information about specific weeds.)

TIPS FOR WORKING OUT WEEDS

• Test a post-emergence herbicide on a small patch before applying it to your whole lawn. Never let it get in nearby beds that contain shrubs or ground covers.
• Be patient when the problem is winter weeds, such as wild onion, in a dormant winter lawn; chemicals work more slowly in cold weather.
• In very weedy lawns, wait until weeds are under control before fertilizing. Apply the herbicide first, and then fertilize three weeks later.

You can pull the occasional weed by hand, but for widespread weed problems you will need to use liquid or granular weedkillers at different times of the year.

ENGINE MAINTENANCE

Unless you have some mechanical skill and experience, you will probably need to take your mower to a professional for a yearly tune-up. The best time to do this is late fall, when the mowing season comes to a close. Ask to have the oil and spark plug changed and the air filter checked and cleaned, if needed.

If you don't plan to have your mower serviced immediately at the end of the growing season, run the mower until the fuel tank is empty. Fuel fumes and residue that build up in stored gasoline can damage engine parts.

Mowing

The cardinal rule of mowing is to mow frequently enough to maintain the desired height, never removing more than one-third of the grass blades in one cutting or more than 1 inch of top growth. The correct mowing height depends primarily on the type of grass you have but is affected also by other factors such as sun, shade, or rainfall. As a general rule, warm-season grasses can take closer clipping than cool-season types. When grass is grown in shade or is seriously stressed by droughts, you should cut it a little higher than usual.

It is usually better to mow high than to cut too low. Mowing a lawn too short can cripple it. When cut too low, grass becomes shallow rooted and more susceptible to drought, requiring much more water to stay green. Close mowing also encourages weeds. A lawn cut at 2 inches or higher, for example, will contain significantly less crabgrass.

RECOMMENDED MOWING HEIGHTS	
Annual Ryegrass	2 to 3 inches
Bahia	2 to 3 inches
Bermuda	
Common	1 to 2 inches
Hybrid	½ to 1 inch
Buffalo Grass	2 to 4 inches
Carpetgrass	1 to 2 inches
Centipede	1½ to 2 inches
Fescues, Fine	2 to 3 inches
Fescue, Tall	2 to 4 inches
Kentucky Bluegrass	1 to 3 inches
Perennial Ryegrass	2 inches
St. Augustine	
Common	3 to 4 inches
Dwarf	1½ to 2½ inches
Zoysia	1 to 2 inches

If you have been away from home and your grass has grown far beyond its best height, set your mower blade very high and mow as usual; then go back a few days later and mow it again with the blade set at the normal level.

Adjusting your mower to the proper cutting height is the single most important item in lawn maintenance. If you mow too close, you'll ruin the lawn.

Taller grass doesn't need to be mowed as often. This is because the rate of blade growth slows as the grass grows taller. A lawn cut at 2½ inches will need less mowing than one cut at 1½ inches.

The quickest way to mow is to go back and forth across the lawn at its widest point, but there are several reasons why you should vary your mowing pattern from time to time. If you always mow in the same pattern, your turf may develop a grain that seems to go in one direction. Also, the places where you turn the mower around at the end of each pass get more wear.

You can follow the fastest pattern when you are short of time, but try out different patterns when you can. Mow diagonally or at right angles to your usual configuration when possible.

The type of lawnmower you use affects the texture of your newly mowed lawn. There are two types of mowers: reel and rotary. Reel mowers do the best job of closely clipping fine-textured Bermuda and Zoysia, but the majority of gardeners prefer rotary mowers.

Using a Rotary Mower

A rotary mower has a twin-edged rapidly spinning blade on a single shaft that cuts by force of impact. Mulching mowers are rotary mowers that cut grass clippings into tiny pieces so that they can be left on the lawn. Rotary mowers come in many different sizes and include riding mowers, self-propelled walk-behind mowers, and walk-behind mowers that you must push. If you have more than an acre of grass, you can probably mow it faster with a riding mower. For intermediate-sized lawns, a self-propelled model that cuts a wide, 22-inch swath may be best. A standard walk-behind mower is sufficient for small lawns.

A rotary mower cuts best when its blade is kept clean and sharp. You can clean the blade by spraying it with a hose, but don't try to sharpen the blade yourself. Because the blade on a rotary mower spins so fast, a slight imbalance caused by uneven sharpening can cause unnecessary strain and wear on the mower. Have the blade professionally sharpened or install a new blade each spring. You can do this easily by turning the mower on its side, removing the lock bolts that hold the blade in place, and installing a new blade. For your safety, be sure to unplug the spark plug before turning your mower over to clean or remove the blade.

A rotary mower cuts by force of impact with a spinning blade; it works best when the blade is sharp and clean.

With the scissorlike action of its whirling blades, a reel mower gives a cleaner cut than a rotary mower, but it is not as easy to maintain.

Using a Reel Mower

A reel mower uses whirling blades attached to its wheels to cut with a scissorlike action. Reel mowers make a much cleaner cut, but they're harder to use and maintain. The mowing height on reel mowers can't be adjusted to cut higher than 2 inches, so they are best for lawn grasses that are always closely mowed. If you want to maintain Bermuda and Zoysia so that your lawn has the texture of a putting green, you will be happiest with a reel mower. Manual push mowers, reel mowers that don't have an engine, are sufficient for cutting very small lawns. To get the best performance from any reel mower, have the blades sharpened once a year. Also, never try to cut grass that is taller than the radius of the wheel.

Bagging Grass Clippings

Many mowers can be equipped with a detachable bag that catches the clippings as they leave the mower. However, if you mow your lawn often, use a mulching mower that will cut the clippings into fine pieces and drop them back onto the lawn. Grass clippings contain plant nutrients that are recycled into the lawn when light layers of the clippings are left to decompose.

Mulching mowers also have bag attachments that come in handy in certain situations. If you are planning an outdoor party, collect the clippings to keep them from getting tracked into your house. You might also bag your clippings when mowing near walkways so that you won't have to sweep when the mowing is done. Finally, if you're fighting lawn diseases or weeds that have flowered and produced seeds, gathering the clippings will prevent the problems from spreading.

A bag or an attachment on your mower will collect clippings, if needed.

Keeping Clean Edges

One of the best ways to make a lawn look neat is to spend a little time edging it. Nothing makes a more immediate impression than a crisp line along the perimeter of the lawn. There are several ways to accomplish this. First, you can install hard plastic edging or design and install a mowing strip. One of the most attractive types of mowing strips is made of mortared bricks, installed level with the ground. The bricks form a track along which the wheels of your mower can run. When you want a mowing strip to separate the lawn from a flowerbed or shrub bed, lay bricks on their sides on the back edge of the strip (photo at right). This design forms a low lip that helps keep mulch and soil inside the planting beds.

Another way to edge your lawn is to use a power edger. Available in gasoline-powered or electric models, this machine is similar to a small mower but with a blade that is short and cuts vertically. You simply guide it along the edges of the lawn as it cuts a deep, narrow trench. An alternative method is to edge by hand with a hoe, a spade shovel, or a manual edger. A manual edger has long handles and a blade that looks like a giant pizza cutter.

The decision to purchase a power edger hinges on how many feet of lawn edge you need to maintain. With a power edger, you can trim the lawn in about the length of time it takes to walk slowly around the edge. Trimming by hand will take considerably longer. If your lawn is bordered by sidewalks, curbs, or a long driveway, a power edger can save you much time and work. Also keep in mind the type of grass that you have. Robust creepers such as Bermuda and St. Augustine need edging more often than centipede, fescue, or Zoysia.

Mortared bricks form a flat mowing strip while bricks laid on their sides help contain the flowerbed.

Watering

A lawn that is properly managed is deep rooted and more resistant to drought stress. One way to encourage deep rooting is to water your lawn well once a week. Applying an inch of water each week should moisten the soil to a depth of 4 to 6 inches, depending on the soil type. If the soil is sandy, you will find that less water is required to moisten it, but the water will be lost more quickly. You can gauge the amount of water you apply by setting tuna or cat food cans at intervals beneath the area covered by the sprinkler. When they are almost full, you have applied an inch of water.

Caring for Your Lawn

Thoroughly watering your lawn encourages deep rooting that makes grass more tolerant of traffic from little feet at play.

Watch for grass blades that begin to curl and take on a blue-gray cast and for footprints that remain in the turf; these are signs of serious drought stress. Don't rush to start watering too soon during periods of drought. During severe summer droughts, it is usually not practical to provide a lawn with enough water to keep it lush and rapidly growing. Instead, give a drought-stressed lawn a weekly soaking just to minimize damage, and postpone any fertilizer applications until rain is forecast.

Raking

Autumn's colorful falling leaves can cause problems for a lawn. During rainy weather, a thick surface layer of leaves can mat down and smother the grass. Large dead patches will appear the following spring. Fallen leaves are particularly troublesome for cool-season grasses such as Kentucky bluegrass, perennial ryegrass, and tall fescue. These grasses emerge from summer dormancy and start growing vigorously in fall. They need plenty of sun during autumn to build up food reserves, which help them weather winter cold.

Leaf litter can also cause the soil to become more acidic. Most grasses grow poorly in highly acidic soils, preferring a near neutral pH. The obvious solution is to diligently remove the leaves as they fall.

You must rake leaves and pine straw from your lawn to keep it from smothering in winter.

Raking is the best method for removing leaves, but you can also use leaf blowers or lawn mowers to do the job. However, leaf blowers usually work better on hard surfaces, such as walkways and driveways, and a lawn mower with a bagger attached won't do a clean sweep of leaves, especially if the leaves are damp. In that situation, you need a trusty rake.

Whether your rake has metal, rubber, or plastic tines, be sure they are flexible so that you can rake either firmly or lightly. A light touch is especially important when raking leaves from a newly seeded lawn. In this case, rake with a gentle, sweeping motion through the grass blades, never scratching the soil's surface.

Removing Thatch

Several types of lawn grasses with stems that creep along the ground tend to develop a thick, undecomposed layer of dead stems, called **thatch.** When thatch accumulates, it keeps grass clippings elevated above the soil so that they decompose slowly and make the problem worse. Thatch also hinders the grass from rooting itself deeply in the soil and can prevent the penetration of rainwater and fertilizers.

To keep thatch from becoming a serious problem, use a hand tool called a thatch rake to comb through the grass in early spring, as soon as the grass begins growing vigorously. For serious thatch problems, you can rent a power rake for the job. If thatch is a recurrent problem in your lawn, you may be overfertilizing. Try fertilizing less, and switch to an organic fertilizer that encourages soilborne microorganisms, which help break down organic matter, such as thatch. In warm climates, such as Florida, where thatch can be especially troublesome, spread a ¼- to ½-inch layer of compost over the lawn in spring to help speed decomposition.

The Healthy Lawn

No lawn looks beautiful every day of the year. Each type of grass has a season when it looks its best, and this is the time when your lawn will be worth all the attention it demands. If you have matched the right grass to the site and have given it proper care, your lawn should improve year after year.

A thatch rake used early in the growing season helps prevent thatch from becoming too thick.

Getting Started with Ground Covers

Ground covers will add texture, color, and richness to your landscape. Use them to create special visual effects or to work as green carpets in shade, on slopes, and in spots where grass will not grow.

Ground covers are tough plants that thrive with little care when you place them in suitable sites. They bring lively color and texture to any part of a landscape and are especially valuable for filling in problem areas where lawn grasses can't survive. For dramatic effect, plant ground covers in large masses or broad borders where their leaf color and texture create a blanket that contrasts with an adjacent lawn or plants.

You can also use ground covers to fill small, difficult spaces, such as strips between an entry walkway and a wall or gaps between stones in a patio floor. Showy ground covers such as variegated pachysandra or elegant ferns are perfect for these high-visibility areas. In very small yards, the right ground cover can serve as a low-maintenance alternative to a lawn.

Ground covers play an important role in landscape design. Because they combine easily with a wide variety of trees and shrubs, evergreen ground covers can tie the landscape together into a unified whole. For example, you can pair a ground cover with a grouping of shrubs and use the same ground cover in another part of your yard around the base of existing trees. The ground cover creates a pattern in the landscape by adding a common texture and color to diverse groups of plants.

The bold textures and colors of evergreen ground covers may be used to frame shapely lawns, accentuate straight or curving lines, or emphasize walkways and driveways. When you use ground covers as edgings, try to make the planting as broad as possible. The lush texture of ground covers is most striking when the plants are featured in wide bands rather than in long, narrow ribbons.

Masses of evergreen holly fern and mondo grass brightened by pink impatiens cover more than half of this shady front lawn.

Matching Ground Covers to the Site

The term ground cover describes the way these plants are used in the landscape. Ground covers include vines, such as ivy, spreading perennials, such as ajuga and dianthus, low shrubs, such as junipers, and a few grasslike plants, such as liriope and mondo grass. As you will see in the Ground Cover Profiles beginning on page 79, each ground cover has strengths that suit it to particular uses and site conditions. But, despite variations in growth habits, all evergreen ground covers have the ability to blanket the garden's floor year-round. Within two years after being planted at the proper spacing, ground cover plants should spread to form a continuous mass of color and texture.

The ground covers discussed in this book are evergreen in most parts of the South. In addition, there are also many ground cover plants that die back to the ground in winter. These ground covers are useful for working into mixed borders, for bringing color to woodland paths, or for combining with larger perennials and bulbs. But evergreen ground covers are as permanent as a lawn, serving as ever-present landscape elements that add texture and unify your yard during every season of the year.

If you choose ground covers that are suited to the sun and soil available to them, you will have little problem turning them into attractive accents for your lawn.

English ivy serves as an evergreen border for this winter lawn, most of which will be shaded in summer.

Light. Ground covers have clear preferences for either sun or shade. Bearberry cotoneaster, dianthus, and junipers, for example, are sun-loving plants that will become thin and leggy when grown in shade. Ground covers that prefer shade, such as Japanese ardisia and Japanese pachysandra, will fade to a sickly yellow color when exposed to too much sun. There is an extensive selection of ground cover plants, and you're sure to find several excellent choices for any light exposure.

Soil. The success or failure of a ground cover is affected by the soil in which it is planted. Rich, moist soil is crucial for ferns and pachysandra, while cotoneasters and junipers need drier, well-drained soils.

Choosing Ground Covers

To cover a large area, you will need many individual ground cover plants. If you have selected a popular ground cover, such as common periwinkle, liriope, or mondo grass, check with family, friends, and neighbors before you buy. They might have plants to share, provided you are willing to dig them. Dig plants carefully, leaving some of the roots intact, and keep these roots constantly moist until you replant the ground cover in your yard.

Type of plants. If you go shopping for your ground cover plants, you may find them as rooted cuttings, as bare-root bundles, or as transplants planted in large flats. Some ground covers are sold only in individual containers. Inspect the plants carefully, buying only those that appear healthy.

Planting season. Early fall is a prime planting season in the South; ground cover plants set out in autumn have sufficient time to develop new roots before spring growth begins. Although fall plantings will need watering in most areas, once established, they won't need extra water where rains are frequent. Spring is the season of growth for most ground cover plants, so early spring is the second-best time to establish new plantings. A few ground covers, such as ivy and liriope, are so vigorous and hardy that they may be planted throughout winter in many locations, provided the plants are well rooted. Don't plant ground covers in summer; if you do, you will have to provide constant irrigation to keep the plants alive.

Less than a year after planting, this mondo grass forms a flowing ground cover. Within three years it will grow into a tight, windswept sea of green.

Preparing To Plant Ground Covers

Preparing the planting bed is crucial to the success of ground covers. You will want to eliminate weeds and be sure that the soil is loose and moist before planting.

Clearing Weeds

Once you have selected an area you want to plant with a ground cover, remove existing weeds and grasses. In large areas mostly covered with weeds, you can spray the ground with a nonselective herbicide, such as Roundup. First, outline the area by laying out a flexible garden hose, or use a can of spray paint to paint the outline on the ground.

You might need to spray an herbicide two or three times several weeks apart to kill stubborn weeds and grasses such as nutgrass or common Bermuda. Allow time for it to work before you start preparing the bed. You may also need to dig weeds by hand in areas next to shrubs or in any areas where drift from the herbicide could cause damage. Be sure to dig or till deeply to remove the entire roots of weeds.

If you prepare a site in late summer for fall planting, you can kill existing weeds and grasses in sunny areas by covering them with a sheet of clear plastic for six weeks. Secure the plastic with boards, stones, or bricks to help hold the heat underneath and to keep the plastic from blowing away.

Preparing the Soil

Take the time to prepare your soil so that the plants' roots will spread properly. Till the soil 4 to 6 inches deep. If the ground is dry, water it thoroughly and wait a night before tilling. Most ground covers quickly develop new roots if the soil is amended with organic matter, such as leaf mold, peat moss, or rotted bark. If your soil is hard and compacted,

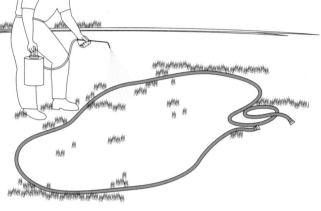

Use a garden hose to mark a new ground cover bed; then spray an herbicide inside the outline to kill the existing grass.

GROUND COVER SPACING

Follow the spacing guidelines given below for some of the most popular evergreen ground covers. The plants should create a solid cover in two to three years; however, growth will vary according to soil type, fertilization, and irrigation.

Ground Cover	Recommended Spacing
Ajuga (*Ajuga reptans*)	8 inches
Ardisia, Japanese (*Ardisia japonica*)	6 to 8 inches
Ivy, English (*Hedera helix*)	14 to 18 inches
Lenten rose (*Helleborus orientalis*)	14 to 18 inches
Liriope (*Liriope species*)	12 inches
Mondo grass (*Ophiopogon japonicus*)	6 inches
Periwinkle, common (*Vinca minor*)	12 inches
Star jasmine, Japanese (*Trachelospermum asiaticum*)	24 inches

mix in coarse sand as well. Add a starter fertilizer that will encourage root development. As you work the soil, rake out any small weeds or grasses that may revive and give you trouble later.

On slopes where tilling is not practical and could cause erosion, dig individual planting holes after all weeds have died. Add a small amount of controlled-release fertilizer to each planting hole. When working on eroded slopes, keep some extra topsoil handy for filling in between plants.

Alternate spacing marks on opposite edges of a 2 x 4 to help line up sprigs.

Planting Ground Covers

Planting ground covers involves the same procedures as setting out a mass of small transplants or a number of small shrubs. Space plants in a gridlike pattern (as shown below), so that each row of plants is offset from the one before it. This will make your planting look unified and will allow your ground cover to fill in evenly. You may mark spacing on a 2 x 4, alternating your marks on the opposite edge of the board (as shown in photo at left). This will help you line up your plants in a gridlike pattern.

Set ground cover plants the same distance from each other in a gridlike pattern to fill the space more uniformly.

Full pots of clump-forming ground covers such as liriope or mondo grass will go further if you divide plants before setting them out. To do this, shop carefully for pots that are full of plants or dig clumps from a friend's garden. Pull plants apart to separate the tight clumps into several divisions. Often such plants will be so crowded that roots grow through the holes in the bottom of the pot. Trim protruding roots, and push on the bottom of the container to free the plant. Use sharp pruning shears or scissors to cut off up to half of the roots. This will make the clump easier to divide and plant and will promote new root growth. Sometimes a sharp knife is needed to divide old clumps of liriope.

Water the transplants well before you begin. As you work, do not allow the divisions taken from pots or the garden to dry out. Place the divisions you aren't working with in a shady spot, and cover them with pine straw or a damp towel to protect the cut roots until you are ready to plant.

Working around Roots

When planting ground covers beneath shade trees, you will need to work around tree roots, which are often widely spread out. Avoid cutting large roots—this may weaken the tree and make it susceptible to soilborne diseases. Instead, use a small spade or trowel to find planting pockets between tree roots. Enrich these open pockets with organic matter, and then go back and blanket the entire area with a 1-inch-deep layer of good topsoil.

Set out your ground cover plants, and water them well. Don't be tempted to pile the soil more deeply, as this can suffocate the tree roots. One inch of soil followed by 1 inch of finely ground bark mulch is enough. Any more than this may injure your tree. If necessary, enclose the bed with a hard edging of brick, stone, or another edging material to help hold the bed in place.

When removing root-bound ground covers from their containers, you may need to cut the protruding roots.

To establish small ground cover plants around the roots of large trees, plant them with a trowel. Eventually they will grow together to hide tree roots.

A blanket of mulch will keep weeds from sprouting until ground covers can grow together to form a solid cover.

Mulching after Planting

After planting, mulch your ground cover with 2 to 3 inches of mulch, such as bark nuggets, pine straw, or shredded bark. In addition to controlling weeds, the mulch will keep the soil moist and cool, which will help your new plants grow quickly.

When planting shrubby ground covers such as cotoneasters or junipers on gentle slopes, you may want to use a landscape fabric between the plants or pine straw mulch which knits together and doesn't wash away as easily as bark. Or, mulch over the bare soil lightly with wheat straw, apply water to soften the straw, and then add a second mulch of pine straw. The wheat straw will knit itself into the soil to help hold the slope, and the pine straw will make the whole planting look neat while keeping it free of weeds.

Watering Well

Unless heavy rain is expected, thoroughly soak the new planting using a sprinkler. In addition to providing much-needed moisture for the small plants, heavy watering will settle the soil and mulch, which will aid in the development of new roots. If the weather is dry after planting, water every two or three days or as often as needed to keep the soil constantly moist but not soggy.

Caring for Ground Covers

Part of the appeal of any ground cover is that, once established, it blankets the earth with handsome foliage that grows low to the ground. The colors and textures of ground covers offer a brilliant complement to nearby lawn grasses, but like any plants they need proper care. As ground cover plantings mature and the plants develop deeper, more extensive root systems, they usually require less maintenance. Mature plantings also have denser foliage. If you use evergreen ground covers, the dense foliage hinders weeds, which need good light exposure to sprout and grow.

During the first year after planting any ground cover, you will need to check its progress every few weeks. Plants that show little new growth or are very slow to fill in the spaces between them may be lacking water, fertilizer, or mulch. Because setting out a large mass of ground cover plants involves a substantial investment in plants and time, you should always try to identify problems early, while you still have a good chance of setting things right.

Almost all ground covers should fill in nicely by the end of their second summer in the ground. From then on, your ground covers should flourish with only occasional watering, fertilizing, and weed control, although some may have trouble bouncing back after stressful periods of drought or cold.

The maintenance requirements of a ground cover decrease as the planting matures into a solid color of green foliage.

Mature ground covers such as this common periwinkle make a striking addition to the landscape.

Drip irrigation or a soaker hose provides a convenient way to water new plantings.

Ground cover plantings such as this liriope and mondo grass will start to fill in during the first growing season.

Watering

Ground cover plantings start out with very skimpy roots. Until a thick tangle of roots develops, they may show little new growth above the ground. Water will encourage growth and help keep the soil soft so that new roots can spread quickly.

Because ground covers need regular watering for only a short period, a sprinkler is a convenient way to provide moisture to a mass of plants. Keep the sprinkler on long enough to soak the ground thoroughly; applying 1 inch of water per watering will moisten the soil 4 to 5 inches deep. (See page 39 for information on how to measure.) Brief waterings that dampen only the top of the soil encourage new roots to form close to the surface, where they may dry out quickly on hot days. Ground covers planted beneath large trees must compete with thirsty tree roots for water; water these plants frequently to help them become established. Or you may want to consider planting ground covers under trees in the fall, when most trees take up very little soil moisture.

Ground covers planted on a slope are difficult to water with sprinklers, for the water tends to wash down the incline. On sloping sites, hide a black soaker hose beneath the mulch so that water will seep slowly to the roots of the plants. You can remove it easily once the ground cover is established.

Of course, you can always handwater any ground cover planting, though this can require a lot of time in hot, dry weather. Plan to handwater only those plants that are water misers by nature, such as cotoneasters or junipers. Ferns, Japanese pachysandra, and other ground covers that prefer moist conditions are better served with drip irrigation or well-placed sprinklers.

Fertilizing

A few ground covers, such as liriope and mondo grass, require very little fertilizer once they are established in appropriate soil. However, most ground covers will show better color and vigor if they are lightly fertilized with a controlled-release fertilizer such as 12-6-6 in early spring before growth begins. Spring fertilization is especially beneficial for very leafy ground covers, including Japanese ardisia, Japanese pachysandra, and Japanese star jasmine. Plants growing in porous, sandy soils in locations that receive heavy rain usually need more fertilizer because the rainwater washes nutrients from the soil.

Soil amendments such as compost also provide plant nutrients, adding the organic matter that some ground covers prefer. Ferns, Japanese pachysandra, and other ground covers suited to shade often like rich soil that holds moisture well. To help maintain this type of soil over time, spread a 1- to 2-inch layer of rotted manure or compost over the soil between the plants in either spring or fall.

Because ground covers have low fertilizer requirements, you should look into other possible causes if a ground cover grows poorly or shows yellowing leaves. Too much sunlight can cause some shade-loving plants to develop pale, yellow leaves, and extremely cold winter temperatures can damage ground cover foliage. Soil pH can also affect the plants' growth. Some soils in the Southeast tend to be very acidic, and some Southwestern soils are very alkaline. A soil pH that is extremely high or extremely low may cause nutrients to become tied up in the soil chemistry and be unavailable to plants. Test your soil's pH using an inexpensive test kit available at most garden centers. If you have a soil test done by a professional, a pH test is part of the routine soil analysis. (See page 32 for more information about soil tests.)

Grooming

Some ground covers always look neat and handsome, while others benefit from occasional trimming. Ground covers that produce flowers, including ajuga and dianthus, will regain their carpetlike texture quickly if you trim off the dead flowers after they fade. Spring is the best time to groom most other ground covers, since cold winter weather can leave the previous year's foliage looking ragged and worn. Removing dead leaves makes the planting look better and clears the way for new growth.

Wait until you see signs of new growth to trim ivy, Japanese pachysandra, and other ground cover plants; new foliage needs to fill open spots quickly to prevent weeds from emerging. However, you should trim liriope and mondo grass in late winter before new growth appears or the new blades will be ragged on the tips. Whether you use pruning shears, a nylon-string trimmer, or your lawnmower set at its highest setting to clean up damaged stems, be careful not to cut into the plants' crowns. Fertilize and water after any severe trimming to stimulate the plants to bounce back promptly.

To keep mature junipers well groomed, remove ragged foliage once or twice a year.

Vining ground covers, such as Japanese star jasmine, knit together in a dense mat that will need edging several times a year along walkways.

Keeping Neat Edges

Spreading ground covers often need to be trimmed to maintain neat edges along walkways and other hard surfaces. The thin woody stems of ivy, common periwinkle, and Japanese star jasmine can be trimmed quickly with a power edger or by hand, using pruning shears. The cut stems that are exposed after you edge any ground cover will be covered within a few weeks by attractive new foliage. Some gardeners like to severely prune the edges of these ground covers in spring, since the new foliage that replaces the old often shows interesting shades of green and always looks vibrant and healthy. Because some of the larger spreading junipers such as Parsons juniper don't look good when edged, you should plant them far enough from the edge so that they will just barely reach it at maturity.

Managing Weeds

Woody tree and shrub seedlings that sprout beneath a cover of foliage and mulch must be removed periodically. Because these plants usually grow from tough, woody roots, you will need to dig or pull them out while they're young and the soil is moist. Use a knife or a weeding tool with a long, sharp blade to cut their roots a few inches below the soil's surface before pulling up the plants. If you cut them at the soil line, they will often regrow.

Weeds that invade ground cover plantings can be a serious problem. It is very difficult to get rid of Bermuda grass, thistles, or other weeds with extensive roots when they grow among ground covers. Because most herbicides used to control weeds will also damage ground covers, pull weeds early and often and keep the ground covered with a thick mulch to discourage newcomers. You can prevent

Newly planted junipers need regular attention so that weeds do not take hold between their woody, creeping stems. Once the plants grow together, weeds are less of a problem.

some weeds from sprouting by sprinkling a pre-emergence herbicide, such as Treflan, in the bed before you mulch; do this in late winter and late summer.

Rejuvenating Old Plantings

Ground covers that have served as permanent features for many years can become so thick that they show little attractive new growth. You can often rejuvenate old plantings of ivy, Japanese star jasmine, and other ground covers by mowing over them in spring with the mower set very high, pulling any weeds or dead plants, and gently raking off the dead leaves. Then fertilize, water, and mulch the planting. Vigorous new growth should soon appear. Ajuga and other ground covers that spread by forming thick bunches can be reworked by digging out the oldest crowns to make room for younger ones.

Propagating Ground Covers

You can propagate most ground covers by simply digging them up and transplanting to a new location. Some, such as periwinkle, form new plants from stems that develop roots wherever they touch the ground. Others, liriope being the most notable, multiply by forming thick bunches. Dig up plants you want to move when the soil is damp, and try to leave some soil attached to the roots. Transplant as soon as possible, and water well.

To protect stem cuttings from drying, cover them with an inverted jar.

You can also propagate certain ground covers by taking cuttings in midsummer and rooting them in pots. To help cuttings from cotoneaster, ivy, Japanese pachysandra, and wintercreeper develop roots quickly, remove all but the topmost leaves from 6-inch-long cuttings. Dip the ends in rooting hormone powder, available at garden centers, and plant 4 inches deep in pots filled with any good potting soil. To maintain high humidity around the planted cuttings, cover them with an inverted glass jar or with a clear plastic lid made to fit over a seed-starting flat. As long as the potted cuttings are not exposed to sun, you can also keep them damp by draping a piece of clear plastic over a group of pots; just be sure the plastic does not touch the cuttings.

Place the container with the new cuttings in a shady place outdoors. Water enough so that the soil remains moist but not soggy. Mist the cuttings with a fine spray of water if they show signs of drying. Remove the clear covering when the plants begin producing new growth, and gradually cut back on watering. Cuttings taken in spring and summer are usually ready to set out in two to three months.

Plant Hardiness Zone Map

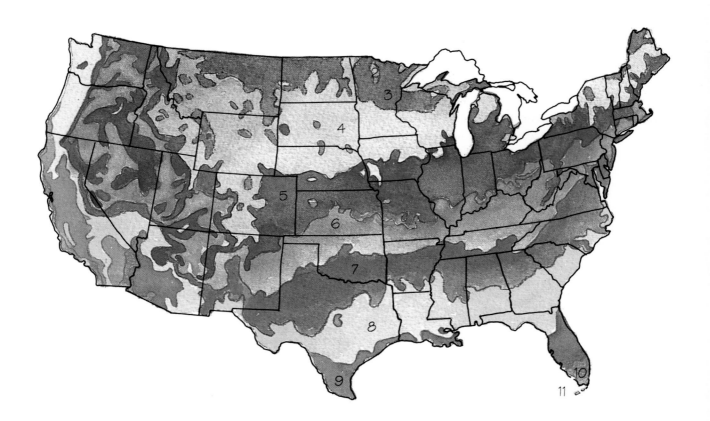

The United States Department of Agriculture has charted low temperatures throughout the country to determine the ranges of average low readings. The map above is based loosely on the USDA Plant Hardiness Zone Map, which was drawn from these findings. It does not take into account heat, soil, or moisture extremes and is intended as a guide, not a guarantee.

The southern regions of the United States that are mentioned in this book refer to the following:

Upper South: Zone 6

Middle South: upper region of Zone 7 (0 to 5 degrees minimum)

Lower South: lower region of Zone 7 and upper region of Zone 8 (5 to 15 degrees minimum)

Coastal South: lower region of Zone 8 and upper region of Zone 9 (15 to 25 degrees minimum)

Tropical South: lower region of Zone 9 and all of Zone 10 (25 to 40 degrees minimum)

Zone 2	-50 to -40°F
Zone 3	-40 to -30°F
Zone 4	-30 to -20°F
Zone 5	-20 to -10°F
Zone 6	-10 to 0°F
Zone 7	0 to 10°F
Zone 8	10 to 20°F
Zone 9	20 to 30°F
Zone 10	30 to 40°F
Zone 11	above 40°F

Lawn Grass Profiles

The lawn grasses described in the following pages were selected by the garden editors at *Southern Living* for their dependability and beauty in the garden. They are also the most popular and reliable lawn grasses for home landscapes. You will find most of these grasses for sale at garden centers as either seed, plugs, or sod.

Arranged alphabetically by common name, these profiles include a description of each grass, information about planting and care, and ways that you can best use each grass in your landscape. Most grasses are planted alone, but a few are mixed with other types of grass. Warm-season grasses, which are dormant in summer, are almost always planted alone. Cool-season grasses, all of which can be started from seed, are often mixed with other cool-season species. These grasses that often are used together in the cooler locations of the upper South are discussed in Cool-Season Mixtures. Critical to your success with any lawn grass is knowing which grasses are adapted to your locale and what type of soil and sunlight each grass needs. You will find this information, as well as troubleshooting tips and solutions, in the profiles.

For a quick summary of each grass, refer to the *At a Glance* box that accompanies every profile. This box will give you the major features of the grass, including the seasons in which it looks its best, the preferred mowing height, and the recommended planting method.

Selecting the right lawn grass for your site and giving the grass the care and maintenance it needs will assure its beauty and durability.

Annual Ryegrass

Annual ryegrass offers winter color for dormant lawns.

Very quick to sprout and grow, annual ryegrass—also called Italian or Oregon ryegrass—is a cool-season grass often used to provide temporary green color in warm-season lawns that become dormant in winter. In all but the coolest climates, annual ryegrass dies out in early summer, for it cannot survive hot weather.

In the Landscape

Any warm-season grass can be overseeded with annual ryegrass in the fall, but the best grasses for overseeding are Bermuda, carpetgrass, and centipede, which have enough space between the blades to allow the seeds to reach the ground easily. Because annual ryegrass requires regular mowing during the winter, planting and maintaining it as a wintergreen grass is recommended only for landscapes that need lively green color. Annual ryegrass is also used as a temporary cover on slopes that are likely to erode during heavy winter rains.

Different Selections

Annual ryegrass is widely available in bulk bags at retail stores. A related species, perennial ryegrass (see profile on page 66) does not grow as quickly as annual ryegrass, but it, too, may be used for overseeding dormant warm-season lawns in the fall.

Planting and Care

The biggest challenge in growing annual ryegrass in an established warm-season lawn is getting the seeds to grow into a uniform stand. (Individual plants grow into tall tufts that do not spread.) Germination is best when the seeds are in firm contact with the soil. To give the seeds better access to the soil, mow the grass as closely as possible without injuring it. Do this in late summer or as it begins to go dormant in the fall. Collect the clippings in a bagger, or rake them from the lawn. Then use a seeder to distribute the ryegrass seeds evenly. Use a sprinkler to keep the seeded area moist until the seeds germinate. Heavy rains can move the seeds into crevices or pockets, which will result in scattered tufts of green all winter. Water regularly until the seeds sprout. Later, you only need to water when the weather is dry. As soon as the ryegrass seeds germinate, fertilize lightly with a winterizer fertilizer such as 8-8-25 to encourage strong growth and safeguard the health of the dormant grass.

Bahia

Bahia, a somewhat coarse warm-season grass from South America, adapts well to poor, infertile sites and requires little maintenance beyond regular mowing until it goes dormant in winter. Individual plants spread by developing short rhizomes and stolons. Bahia grows best in the sandy soils of Florida and the coastal portions of Zones 8, 9, and 10.

In the Landscape

Bahia can handle strong sun and dry soil and also adjusts reasonably well to partial early morning or late afternoon shade. Bahia's assets include deep, extensive roots, scant fertilizing requirements, and very high resistance to most pests. Its biggest problems are its rough texture and many tall seedheads which need frequent mowing. Since Bahia does not have the fine texture of other lawn grasses, it is usually the choice only for places where a lawn is needed and no other grass will grow.

Different Selections

Two types of Bahia are easily sown from seed: Argentine and Pensacola. Argentine is dark green and dense; it is often preferred for lawns. Pensacola is slightly lighter in color and is grown along roadsides and in other low-maintenance areas. Both of these selections produce numerous tall seedheads, although those of Pensacola are the tallest, reaching 18 inches in height. Wilmington, another selection, produces fewer seeds and is planted mostly from plugs.

Planting and Care

Bahia is usually started from seed. The best time to sow Bahia seed is early to midspring. You will need 5 to 10 pounds of seed to plant 1,000 square feet. Distribute the seeds evenly, and rake lightly to settle the seeds into the soil. Keep the soil moist until seeds germinate, and continue to water mature grass once a week during the growing season.

Fertilize established Bahia once a year, in early summer, using a balanced controlled-release fertilizer. Mow as needed to keep the grass under 3 inches high and to prevent the growth of tall seedheads. In spring and summer, you may need to mow every five days. A rotary mower will slice off the seedheads provided the blade is kept sharp. To ensure a thick lawn, reseed bare spots or thin areas in spring.

Troubleshooting

Bahia may be bothered by dollar spot, a fungal disease, and by mole crickets. See pages 119 and 121 for more information.

Bahia is a rugged grass that grows well in poor, sandy soils.

AT A GLANCE
❖
BAHIA
Paspalum notatum

Type: warm season
Green season: spring to fall
Dormant season: winter
Light: full sun to light shade
Soil: sandy
Water: low
Planting method: seed, sod
Mowing height: 2 to 3 inches
Range: Zones 8 to 10
Pests: dollar spot, mole crickets
Remarks: coarse texture, numerous tall seedheads

Bermuda

Bermuda has the finest texture of all Southern lawn grasses.

AT A GLANCE
❖
BERMUDA
Cynodon dactylon

Type: warm season

Green season: spring to fall

Dormant season: winter

Light: full sun

Soil: well drained

Water: low-common; medium-hybrid

Planting method: sod, seed, plugs, sprigs

Mowing height: 1 to 2 inches

Range: Zones 6 to 10

Pests: chinch bugs, dollar spot, white grubs

Remarks: highly wear resistant

Common Bermuda is one of the most widely used grasses in the South. Exceptionally drought tolerant and quick to establish from seed, it can form a solid lawn in just one year. Because it also tolerates salt spray, it is suitable for growing near the beach. However, common Bermuda is not very cold hardy and becomes thin and stringy even in slight shade. Moreover, it spreads aggressively by *rhizomes*, (stems that grow at the soil surface) readily invading flowerbeds and shrub beds, where it becomes difficult to control.

Fortunately, common Bermuda has been improved by hybridization to create selections that are less weedy. These hybrids feature finer texture and better color and are much slower to spread where they are not wanted. However, the improved Bermuda grasses require more fertilization and supplemental water during dry weather than common Bermuda to bring out their beautiful texture and wear resistance. And these improved grasses are not always winter hardy in the upper South. Unlike common Bermuda, most hybrids are not available in seed but must be started from sod, plugs, or sprigs, which adds to the expense of having a Bermuda lawn. But when an improved Bermuda lawn is properly maintained, it is one of the most beautiful grasses for Southern lawns.

In the Landscape

Bermuda, both common and hybrid, requires full sun and good drainage. A warm-season grass, Bermuda stays vibrantly green from midspring to late fall and becomes a soft carpet of light buff during the winter months. When framed with an evergreen ground cover, a Bermuda lawn can look as pretty in winter as it does during the summer. If you do not like a buff lawn in winter, overseed with perennial ryegrass in early fall.

Sunny areas that must withstand foot traffic or wear and tear from active children are good places for a Bermuda lawn. But common Bermuda is extremely invasive, so avoid using it in any areas close to garden beds. And even when growing the better-behaved hybrid Bermudas, be sure to install hard edging materials to keep the grass from creeping where you do not want it to grow.

Different Selections

For color, texture, and pest resistance, it is hard to beat Tifway (also known as T-419) and Tifway II, two hybrid Bermuda strains developed in Tifton, Georgia. While not quite as fine in texture as some of the hybrid Bermudas grown on golf courses, these two strains are relatively easy to maintain with regular mowing and fertilization. Once established, they stand up to drought and heavy traffic. Tifway produces few, if any, viable seeds and must be planted from sod. Sahara, Sonesta, and Yuma are improved turf-quality Bermudas that can be started from seed but are finer textured and make better lawn grass than common Bermuda.

Not all hybrid Bermudas are slow spreaders, and some are almost as invasive as common Bermuda. Midiron and Vamont, for example, are very tough and cold tolerant but are extremely aggressive as well.

Planting and Care

Common Bermuda can be planted from seed or sprigs, but most hybrid Bermudas are planted from sod. Make sure the site is absolutely smooth before laying Bermuda sod, for the ideal mowing height is only 1 inch, and any bumps will be scalped at this height. A reel mower will produce the best results, but a rotary mower with a sharp blade does a good job, too. You can allow the clippings to decompose on the lawn as long as you mow when the grass is no higher than 2 inches. When mowing overgrown Bermuda, collect the clippings in a bagger and use them as mulch in other parts of your landscape. Plan to mow about once a week during summer, except during periods of drought. Mow hybrid Bermudas about 1 inch high; mow common Bermuda 2 inches high.

When spring or early summer is unusually dry, be prepared to water your Bermuda lawn. Provide 1 inch of water per week (1½ inches for porous, sandy soils). Signs of drought stress in Bermuda include a blue-gray color and curled or folded blades.

About two weeks after the grass turns green in spring, begin fertilizing your Bermuda lawn. If crabgrass and other grassy weeds have been a problem the previous summer, you may want to use a pre-emergence herbicide, applying it slightly earlier in the spring than if you were using fertilizer alone. Unless a soil test indicates otherwise, apply a controlled-release, high-nitrogen lawn fertilizer at regular intervals during the summer. How often you apply depends on the product you use; read the fertilizer label for the recommended rate of application. Most controlled-release fertilizers last two to three months. Switch to a high-potassium fertilizer, such as 6-6-12, for your last fertilization in early fall.

HYBRID VERSUS COMMON BERMUDA

Hybrid Bermuda grasses are an improvement of common Bermuda grass. The main differences between the hybrids and common Bermuda are their texture and the way they are started. The improved, hybrid types have smaller grass blades and create a finer, more closely knit lawn. They are only available from sod, making them much more expensive than common Bermuda, which is usually started from seed.

Some of the better-known hybrids include Tifgreen, Tifton, and Tifway. They are the premier grasses of putting greens on Southern golf courses.

You may see other Bermuda grass sold in seed packages which are not hybrids but are indeed improvements over common Bermuda. Sahara, Sonesta, and Yuma are three such selections. Although not as fine textured as the golf course quality hybrids, they still have a finer texture than common Bermuda.

Every two to three years, your Bermuda lawn may start to feel spongy under your feet, a sign that thatch has built up at the soil's surface. If the thatch layer is more than ½ inch thick, it can prevent water and fertilizer from reaching the grass's roots. You can remove thatch with a thatch rake or power rake. If your lawn is more than 1,000 square feet, rent a power rake to make this job go faster. For best results, follow up the dethatching with a scheduled fertilizer application and a thorough watering.

Troubleshooting

If you fertilize and mow your Bermuda lawn properly, weeds should not be much of a problem. If small outbreaks occur, you may pull the weeds by hand or spot-spray with a ready-to-use bottled weedkiller. For large outbreaks, you will need to apply weedkiller over the entire area. (See page 35 for more information about weedkillers.) Promptly replant the disturbed area with plugs of grass from the edge of your lawn.

White grubs, which are the larvae of many different types of beetles such as June beetles and Japanese beetles, feed on the roots of several grasses, including Bermuda. If you notice places where the grass is struggling and identify white grubs feeding on your lawn's roots, you need to take action. Apply a recommended pesticide, or combination fertilizer-grub control product, in early or late summer, when the grubs are closest to the surface. Another way to get rid of white grubs is to apply a beneficial fungus called milky spore disease, which is usually available from mail-order sources. You must spray it over a very large area to control enough grubs to keep them from coming back into the lawn. If some of your neighbors have grub problems as well, you may want to treat all of the lawns at the same time. See page 122 for more information on these pests.

Chinch bugs may attack a Bermuda lawn. They are usually worse during hot, dry weather. Another problem for Bermuda is dollar spot, a fungal disease. See pages 119 and 120 for more information.

Bermuda is a vigorous grass that grows quickly in warm weather.

Buffalo Grass

Buffalo grass is as tough as it sounds, yet soft on bare feet. The original grass rippled across the Great Plains in airy, blue-green waves. In recent years, improved selections of this native, warm-season grass have become popular as lawn grasses in the arid parts of the South, including Texas and Oklahoma. New plantings are being evaluated in the more humid climates and acidic soils of Georgia and South Carolina, but the long-term performance of this drought-tolerant prairie grass in these comparatively high rainfall areas is not known. In dry soils, where it grows well, buffalo grass forms a fine-textured lawn that requires no supplemental water, very little fertilizer, and only monthly mowing during the summer.

In the Landscape

Buffalo grass grows best in dry, heavy soils that are neutral or slightly alkaline. It flourishes in full sun but will tolerate partial afternoon shade in areas where the summers are hot. This grass creeps along the ground slowly and will require edging once or twice during the summer if grown near walkways and flowerbeds. Tremendously tolerant of heat and cold, buffalo grass becomes a tan carpet in winter when it is dormant but turns green again in spring. It is hardy in Zones 4 to 7.

Different Selections

Buffalo grass seed is widely available in areas where it is grown, but the selections that can be grown from seed also produce many prickly seedheads. Seed-propagated selections need frequent mowing to keep the seedheads from maturing. New selections developed by the University of Nebraska include one called 609 Buffalo Grass and another named Prairie. These improved turf-type buffalo grass selections can be planted only from sod or plugs but produce comparatively few prickly seedheads. They are definitely superior and worth the extra cost.

Planting and Care

Buffalo grass seed, sod, or plugs are planted just like other lawn grasses, though you must be careful to eliminate all weeds first. This grass is easily injured by herbicides used to control lawn weeds, so wait two weeks after you have used herbicides to kill existing grasses and weeds before you plant buffalo grass. It has no problem with alkaline conditions in which the pH hovers around 7.0 and

Buffalo grass tolerates drought and alkaline soil.

AT A GLANCE
❖
BUFFALO GRASS
Buchloe dactyloides

Type: warm season
Green season: spring to fall
Dormant season: winter
Light: full sun
Soil: well drained, alkaline
Water: low
Planting method: seed, sod, plugs
Mowing height: 2 to 4 inches
Range: Zones 4 to 7
Pests: none specific
Remarks: superior drought and cold tolerance

prefers poor native soil to rich, fertile soil that has been improved prior to planting.

Buffalo grass needs water at planting time and for several weeks afterward. You should sprinkle seeded areas daily and give sodded lawns a thorough initial soaking. Follow with regular watering to keep the soil consistently moist for two weeks after planting. Do not be alarmed if your newly sodded buffalo grass turns brown after planting. At first, buffalo grass sends down new roots before sending up new shoots. With adequate water, it should turn green in about two weeks. The best time to plant either seed or sod is late spring to early summer.

Once established, buffalo grass needs no extra water and should only be fertilized very lightly in early summer, if at all. A fertilizer designed for centipede, such as 15-0-15, is ideal. Too much water and fertilizer will encourage weeds. When neglected, buffalo grass seldom has problems with weeds because few weeds will grow in the dry conditions under which this grass thrives.

If you want a manicured look, mow your buffalo grass at a height of 2 inches but never shorter. Mowing too low or too often can invite weeds. You can also let your buffalo grass grow to its mature height of 6 inches and not mow it at all except in spring when new shoots begin to emerge. For this first spring mowing, set the mower blade at 2 inches, and give the grass a close trim. After that, you can keep mowing it low, let it grow high, or mow it every three to four weeks at about 3 inches.

A wild grass that is native to the Great Plains, buffalo grass can make a handsome lawn.

Carpetgrass

A tropical grass from Central America, carpetgrass survives winter only in the lower South where the soil never freezes. It is used in Florida and along the Gulf Coast, where frequent, heavy rains give it the moisture it requires to grow well. This grass will spread by creeping, but you will need to water and fertilize it regularly to help it form a nicely textured lawn. Its natural color is light to medium green. Carpetgrass looks like centipede in many ways but is better adapted to low, damp sites. It also produces more tall, upright seedheads than centipede. Carpetgrass usually is used only as a last resort for low, wet, shady spots where other warm-season grasses popular in the coastal South do not thrive.

In the Landscape
Carpetgrass grows well in full sun or partial shade, but it must have regular moisture and cannot tolerate salt spray or severe drought. Acidic soil is no problem for carpetgrass, which actually prefers a pH between 4.5 and 5.5. However, because carpetgrass requires frequent mowing in summer, it is best to use it in level, accessible places. It can withstand moderate foot traffic if it receives regular water and fertilizer. For improved winter color, overseed carpetgrass in fall with annual or perennial ryegrass.

Different Selections
Carpetgrass is not generally sold by selection name. This species is a prolific seed producer, and seed germination is usually very high. The seed is sometimes mixed with centipede seed, which is slower to sprout and grow; in this way, the carpetgrass becomes a *nurse crop,* growing to fill in the area until the slower-growing centipede eventually takes over.

Planting and Care
Sow carpetgrass seed in early to midspring. Although carpetgrass will grow in infertile soils, organic matter added to the soil will help retain moisture and improve growth. You will need 3 pounds of seed to plant 1,000 square feet.

Fertilize established carpetgrass after it turns green in spring and again in early summer with a controlled-release fertilizer. Using a rotary mower, mow carpetgrass as needed to keep it under 2 inches high and to control the emergence of seedheads, which are produced continually during the summer. Water during periods of drought.

Carpetgrass is rarely used but serves well on wet, shady sites.

AT A GLANCE
❖
CARPETGRASS
Axonopus affinis

Type: warm season
Green season: spring to fall
Dormant season: winter
Light: full sun to partial shade
Soil: moist, acidic
Water: medium
Planting method: seed
Mowing height: 1 to 2 inches
Range: Zones 8 to 10
Pests: none specific
Remarks: tolerant of wet, poorly drained soil

Centipede

Centipede requires the least maintenance of all the warm-season grasses.

Though hardly a glamorous grass, centipede has many favorable qualities. It grows in highly acidic and poor soils where other grasses fail; it requires less mowing than other grasses; and it needs little fertilizer. On the other hand, it does not have the fine texture or drought tolerance of Bermuda or Zoysia, nor can it handle cold winter weather north of Atlanta or Dallas. But centipede thrives in the thin, sandy soils and hard clays of the lower and coastal South, where it is popular for its low-maintenance requirements and its willingness to grow in full sun or light shade. It has sometimes been called "poor man's grass," but a better nickname might be "easy-care grass."

In the Landscape

Centipede is a warm-season grass that becomes light green in late spring and fades to light brown after frost in late fall. This grass creeps along the ground, but the runners have such shallow roots that you can easily pull them up if they invade your flowerbeds. Centipede cannot tolerate heavy traffic or deep shade but otherwise is adaptable to many landscape situations. This grass, like other warm-season grasses, can be overseeded with a cool-season grass for winter color, as long as the process is done carefully and fertilizer is not used. Centipede grass will decline if overfertilized, so be sure not to apply fertilizer to the overseeded grass. Centipede requires acidic soil, preferring a soil pH of 4.5 to 5.5 to thrive. It will decline at a higher pH.

Different Selections

Centipede seed, sod, or sprigs are not usually sold by selection name. The grass was imported from China in 1916, and with the exception of some efforts to improve its winter hardiness, it has changed little. One brand, Pennspeed, is a seed mix that also contains carpetgrass, which serves as a quick cover until the slower centipede becomes established.

Planting and Care

The easiest way to start centipede is from sod or plugs. You can plant centipede from seed, but it usually takes three years for a seeded centipede lawn to cover completely. To plant a centipede lawn from seed, you will need 1 to 1½ pounds of seed per 1,000 square feet. Late spring is the best time to sow seed; expect it to take two to three weeks to germinate. It is also best to plant either sod or plugs in late spring or a combination of sprigs and seeds. You will need ¾ bushel of sprigs for 1,000 square feet. After planting, keep the area moist for three weeks by sprinkling it twice a day. Do not apply lime or fertilizer to the soil before or after you plant centipede.

During the summer, mow centipede at about 1½ inches. Raise the cutting height to 2 inches during periods of drought. As long as you mow as needed, the grass clippings may be allowed to decompose on the lawn. Fertilize established centipede lawns once a year, in spring, using a fertilizer that contains no phosphorus, such as 15-0-15. A good centipede fertilizer will also contain extra iron. Never feed centipede extra nitrogen to make it turn dark green, for it is naturally a light, apple green color. Centipede that appears yellow may need iron; apply a supplement, such as Ironite or iron sulfate, according to label directions.

Troubleshooting

Centipede is sensitive to many herbicides, so carefully check the label before using any weed-control product on your centipede lawn. Nematodes also can injure centipede, especially during periods of drought; provide regular water during severe dry spells to limit the amount of injury. Chinch bugs are another pest that can attack the grass. See pages 120–121 for more information about these pests.

Two other problems may develop in centipede lawns. One is dead spots that may appear following extremely cold winters. The other is a more complex problem known as centipede decline, which is often related to overfertilization, excessive thatch, or both. It is easier to prevent the buildup of thatch than to remove thatch that has accumulated over time; aggressive dethatching with a power rake can seriously injure a centipede lawn. Instead of letting the thatch build up, rake your dormant centipede lawn in early spring to remove any dead stems and undecomposed clippings. Although some people burn off their centipede grass to get rid of this loose material, burning can injure the roots so seriously that the grass will never grow back the way it should.

Centipede has a coarse texture but makes a handsome, uniform lawn.

Cool-Season Mixtures

Perennial ryegrass is used as a winter grass in the South.

Hot summer weather is so stressful to most cool-season grasses that they are seldom used for lawns in most parts of the middle, lower, and tropical South. Tall fescue, the most heat tolerant of cool-season grasses, is a notable exception. It is the preferred lawn grass for partially shaded lawns in the middle and upper South and some areas of the lower South.

This does not mean that you should forget about using other cool-season grasses in your lawn. In the mountains and plateaus of the upper South, cool-season grasses, including Kentucky bluegrass and perennial ryegrass, can be used to create breathtaking lawns. Kentucky bluegrass, perennial ryegrass, tall fescue, and a few other cool-season grasses may be grown alone or in various combinations. You will find the seeds for these grasses packaged in mixtures (combinations of different types of grass) or blends (combinations of different selections of the same type of grass). Similar mixtures and blends are often sold as mature sod.

To understand how mixtures or blends might work in your yard, first read about the major cool-season grasses and how they grow. Because tall fescue and Kentucky bluegrass are also widely used as primary lawn grasses by themselves, they are profiled separately on pages 69 and 72, respectively. The other two most common types of cool-season grasses used in mixes, perennial ryegrass and fine fescues, are discussed below.

Perennial Ryegrass

Tremendously tolerant of cold weather, perennial ryegrass is the best grass for overseeding dormant Bermuda to produce a green winter lawn. When used this way in the middle and lower South, perennial ryegrass is rarely perennial, dying out in summer's heat and requiring reseeding in the fall. Perennial ryegrass is basically a tuft-forming grass that spreads only slightly. You can purchase the seed in bags or boxes labeled with a selection name, such as Citation or Manhattan.

The seed of annual ryegrass, a different species, is inexpensive compared with perennial ryegrass seed, but the perennial form is worth the extra cost. Annual ryegrass grows so fast and tall that it needs regular mowing all winter long. Perennial ryegrass grows slowly and will need little mowing until the weather warms in spring. This ryegrass has a fine texture and a dark green color.

In the upper South, perennial ryegrass does not always die out in the summer and is often used in combination with Kentucky bluegrass and tall fescue in seed mixtures and sod. When blended with other grasses, perennial ryegrass produces a lawn that establishes quickly, has outstanding winter color, and is extremely cold hardy.

Fine Fescues

Besides the popular tall fescue, there are several other fescues, collectively called fine fescues, that are included in cool-season seed mixes. Although normally used in smaller quantities than tall fescue, fine fescues are more tolerant of shade than other lawn grasses; therefore, you will often see them in special mixes for shady lawns. Fine fescues are cool-season grasses that struggle in hot climates, so they are not very well suited to the South. They are named for their very thin blade, which gives these grasses a fine texture.

Creeping red fescue *(Festuca rubra)* is a cool-season perennial grass that spreads by forming short rhizomes. It prefers a cool, humid climate such as that of the Pacific Northwest. However, you will find selections of creeping red fescue in shady mixes sold throughout the United States. Flyer is a selection sometimes used for shady areas in the cooler portions of the upper South.

Chewings fescue *(Festuca rubra* var. *commutata)* is similar to creeping red fescue but does not spread by rhizomes. Instead it grows in upright bunches like tall fescue, only with a much finer texture. Even more tolerant of shade than creeping red fescue, Chewings fescue is rarely sold alone but as part of mixes for shade.

Hard fescue *(Festuca longifolia)* is another bunching grass that is used in cool-season mixes. Although not an annual grass, hard fescue is not long lived, but it is included in a few seed mixes for its tolerance to shade and its deep green color.

Seed Mixtures

The appearance of a lawn planted from a mixture of cool-season grass seed slowly changes during the first two years after planting. Although the mixture may contain more than 50-percent Kentucky bluegrass seed, bluegrass takes longer to germinate than either perennial ryegrass or tall fescue. Typically, the perennial ryegrass sprouts first and stabilizes the seedbed; the tall fescue sprouts next and covers the soil with a fuzz of green; and the Kentucky bluegrass appears later and slowly spreads between the other plants. Because all of these grasses grow best in cool weather, the optimum time to plant a cool-season seed

Fine fescues are tolerant of some shade.

AT A GLANCE
❖
FINE FESCUES
Festuca rubra
Festuca rubra var. *commutata*
Festuca longifolia

Type: cool season
Green season: fall to spring
Dormant season: summer
Light: partial sun to shade
Soil: moist, fertile
Water: medium
Planting method: seed
Mowing height: 2 to 3 inches
Range: Zones 3 to 6
Pests: none specific
Remarks: tolerant of shade

mixture is in late summer or early fall when the ground is still warm enough to speed root growth and the growing season for cool-season grasses is just beginning. Keep the seeded area constantly moist for about three weeks. Begin mowing when the grass is 3 inches high to keep the fescue from shading out the Kentucky bluegrass.

Four to six weeks after the seeds germinate, lightly fertilize your newly seeded lawn with a balanced controlled-release lawn fertilizer such as 27-3-6. The following spring, do a soil test to determine what changes in fertilization and adjustments to soil pH are needed.

Planting and Care of Cool-Season Sod

The best cool-season sod is a mixture of fescues, Kentucky bluegrass, and small amounts of perennial ryegrass. When shopping for sod, you may also find less costly fescue-ryegrass mixtures that contain no Kentucky bluegrass. Since neither fescue nor ryegrass creep enough to knit the sod together, fescue-ryegrass sod may be held together with plastic netting. This netting binds the roots together and makes the sod easier to handle and plant. However, there are some disadvantages to netting. When netted sod is planted in high-traffic areas or places where pets are kept, the grass can be damaged so badly that the netting shows through. Exposed netting can be a safety hazard if it catches on shoes. But if you are planting a lawn area that will not receive heavy wear, netting will not pose problems.

You should plant Kentucky bluegrass sod or mixed Kentucky bluegrass-fescue-ryegrass sod in fall. To encourage the bluegrass, monitor the soil's pH closely and keep it between 6.5 and 7.0. Using a balanced controlled-release lawn fertilizer such as 22-4-14, fertilize in fall, and again in late fall with a winter formula such as 18-6-12.

Most mixtures of cool-season grasses have an elegant, fine texture.

Fescue, Tall

The most popular grass for shady or partially shady yards in the middle and upper South is tall fescue. It is the most heat-tolerant of all of the cool-season grasses and is sufficiently cold hardy to withstand severe winter weather. Tall fescue does not creep at all; a tall fescue lawn is made up of millions of individual plants growing in little tufts. The texture of tall fescue is often described as coarse, but newer varieties have narrow leaves that create a finer-textured turf. This grass shows excellent medium-green color, especially during the cooler months when it grows best. If well maintained, a tall fescue lawn can survive heavy wear.

In the Landscape
Tall fescue will grow in sun or shade and makes a beautiful lawn in places that receive filtered sun in summer and full sun in winter. Because this grass does not creep, you can easily prevent it from invading flowerbeds. Tall fescue does require good drainage and grows especially well in lawns that have a very slight slope. This grass is at its best in fall and spring, when it forms a vibrant green carpet that sparkles in the sun.

Different Selections
The most common strain of tall fescue used for lawns is Kentucky-31. Often abbreviated as K-31, this old selection is inexpensive and its seed is widely available. However, improved tall fescues that go by selection names such as Adventure, Apache, Arid, Bonanza, Clemfine, Enviro, Falcon, Finelawn, Olympic, and Rebel II usually produce a better-quality lawn. Compared to these improved tall fescues, Kentucky-31 has much more trouble looking good in hot summer weather. The improved strains are also more successful against crabgrass and other weeds and usually grow better in shade than does Kentucky-31. Most importantly, improved tall fescues have a finer texture and grow lower than Kentucky-31, and they tend to require less frequent mowing.

Improved tall fescues often can be purchased in blends of several selections. Since each selection of tall fescue adapts a little differently to a given site, using one of these blends is usually the best way to ensure a successful lawn. You may find blends created for special situations, such as shade, which capitalize on the strengths of the selections included.

Tall fescue is the most heat and drought tolerant of all the cool-season grasses.

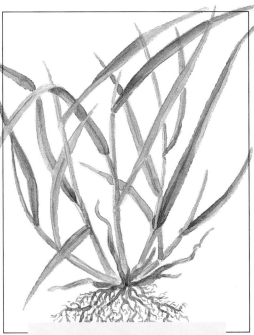

AT A GLANCE
❖
TALL FESCUE
Festuca arundinacea

Type: cool season
Green season: spring, fall
Dormant season: none
Light: sun to partial shade
Soil: fertile, well drained
Water: medium
Planting method: seed, sod
Mowing height: 2 to 4 inches
Range: Zones 4 to 8
Pests: brown patch, snow mold
Remarks: dazzling fall and
    spring color

Tall fescue has a coarse texture and a more upright growth habit than fine fescues.

Planting and Care

Tall fescue is normally planted from seed but is also available as sod. It grows best in fertile, well-drained soil with a pH between 5.5 and 6.5, but it will tolerate more acidic or alkaline conditions. When preparing a site for seeding, remove all weeds (and add lime, if needed) to raise the pH of extremely acidic soil to 5.5 to 6.5. Follow the directions on pages 26 and 27 for seeding lawns. Then lightly mulch with straw. If you apply only a light cover of straw, or about one bale per 1,000 square feet, the fescue will grow through the straw, which will eventually decompose.

The best months to plant tall fescue are September and October. Fallen leaves must be kept from blocking light to new grass; plant as soon as cool weather begins in fall so that the grass will be growing well before you start raking leaves. You can also plant between late February and March, but expect your young grass to struggle in the summer. Tall fescue planted in early spring will usually need more water during its first summer, since the grass will not have developed extensive deep roots by the time hot summer weather begins.

Heat and drought stress often weaken fescue lawns, so reseeding about every third year is recommended. Some people reseed their lawn annually to help keep it lush and thick. To reseed thin fescue, mow the lawn, rake it clean, and reseed the thin spots or the entire lawn with 5 pounds of seed per 1,000 square feet. Rake lightly to help settle the seeds into pockets of exposed soil, and water well. You can also reseed thin fescue lawns in early spring, but they will need careful watering in summer.

Tall fescue should be mowed higher than other lawn grasses, at 2 to 4 inches, depending on the selections as well as the site and the season. Improved types that are bred as dwarf selections will tolerate the closest mowing. Mow higher in dense shade and during periods of drought or heat. As long as you remove no more than one-third of the grass's growth when mowing, the clippings can be left where they fall.

Provide 1 inch of water weekly during dry periods. During severe droughts, tall fescue lawns often become dormant and turn brown. To keep the grass from dying, water weekly. Weekly watering during very hot, dry weather will not make your fescue turn lush and green, but it will keep it alive until cool weather returns.

Fertilize your fescue lawn over a six-month period beginning in September and ending in early February. Fertilizing after mid-March helps the weeds more than the fescue turf and may encourage disease. Use a controlled-release lawn fertilizer. Three light fertilizer applications are much better than a single heavy one. Your goal is to fertilize fescue regularly during its most active period of growth to help it develop the deep roots and thick crowns necessary to get it through the stresses of summer. Since tall fescue does not creep, it never requires dethatching.

Weeds are seldom a problem in fescue lawns that are fertilized properly and that are reseeded when they become thin. However, you can use a pre-emergence herbicide in spring if needed to control crabgrass and other weeds. Be sure to follow label instructions exactly.

Troubleshooting

Warm, wet weather sometimes gives rise to a fungal disease called brown patch, which produces pale brown circles or ovals, often with overlapping edges, in an otherwise green lawn. This disease is rare in fescue lawns that are fertilized only during the cool seasons. A more likely cause of browning in summer is high temperature stress. If water is provided weekly, the grass will survive a torrid summer and begin growing vigorously again in early fall. See page 118 for more information about brown patch.

Tall fescue appreciates a little shade in the South.

Kentucky Bluegrass

Kentucky bluegrass is prized for its color and fine texture.

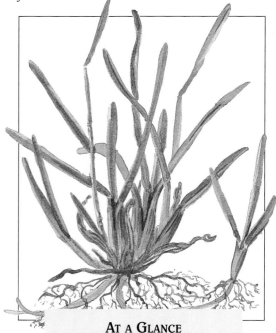

AT A GLANCE
❖
KENTUCKY BLUEGRASS
Poa pratensis

Type: cool season
Green season: fall to spring
Dormant season: midsummer
Light: sun to partial shade
Soil: rich, well drained, near
   neutral
Water: medium
Planting method: seed, sod
Mowing height: 1 to 3 inches
Range: Zones 3 to 7
Pests: brown patch, snow mold
Remarks: very fine texture,
   dark color

A lush, dark blue-green grass, Kentucky bluegrass is the leading lawn grass in many states in the upper South and North. It spreads by sending out slender rhizomes in all directions, which take root along the soil's surface. Bluegrass lawns have a very fine texture.

In the Landscape
Kentucky bluegrass needs excellent drainage, fertile soil with a near-neutral pH, and plenty of light. In cold climates this grass requires full sun, but in Southern landscapes bluegrass likes afternoon shade.

Different Selections
Named bluegrass selections include Adelphi, Baron, and Glade. Huntsville, a selection from Huntsville, Alabama, grows surprisingly well in the middle South. Because bluegrass selections vary slightly in their tolerance of cold, heat, and disease, sowing a blend that contains several selections produces the most versatile turf. Selections also vary in growth habit, with some being more upright and coarse than others. To achieve a uniform look, it is best to purchase a premixed blend. Sod sold as 100-percent bluegrass is almost always a blend of several named selections.

Bluegrass is often combined with fescue and perennial ryegrass in seed mixtures and sod. Landscapers call this sod "blue fescue."

Planting and Care
The best time to sow seed or plant sod is at the end of summer or in early fall. Early spring is the next best, although bluegrass planted in spring will have a more difficult time in summer because the root system is still young when warm weather arrives.

Remove all weeds from the area to be planted, and add compost, manure, or another type of organic matter to create a fertile bed for the grass. If planting seed, you will need 2 to 3 pounds of seed to plant 1,000 square feet. Distribute the seed evenly, and rake lightly to settle the seeds into the soil. Keep the seeded area moist for three weeks to encourage vigorous sprouting.

Fertilize established bluegrass twice a year, in fall and again in early spring, using a controlled-release fertilizer. Check the soil pH every two years, and apply lime if needed to maintain a pH of 7.0.

Troubleshooting
Kentucky bluegrass may be bothered by brown patch. See page 118 for more information about this disease.

St. Augustine

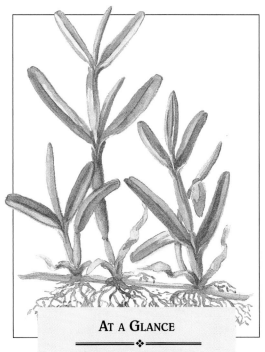

The primary grass of the coastal South, St. Augustine has wide blades and a coarse texture.

The lawn grass of choice for shady spots in the lower South, St. Augustine quickly covers the soil with a dark green carpet. The individual leaves are the broadest of all the lawn grasses, but this grass covers the ground so densely that it never appears coarse or rough. The sheer size of the blades and the vigor of St. Augustine make this grass feel thick and cushiony underfoot.

Unfortunately, St. Augustine can not tolerate very cold winters and will only grow well in Zones 8, 9, and 10 and in the warmer portions of Zone 7.

In the Landscape

St. Augustine is a rugged grass that is completely at home in the hot blazing sun, in alkaline soil, and even along the beach. However, some selections also fare well beneath the thin, high shade of pine trees and in other areas that receive light shade during much of the day. It is an excellent grass for lawns that are often used for outdoor play, since the vigorous runners quickly fill in spots that become damaged or worn. However, the thick *stolons*, or spreading stems, that run along the ground must also be trimmed or edged periodically when they creep into flowerbeds or other areas where they are not wanted. St. Augustine is the primary lawn grass of coastal landscapes as it tolerates alkaline soil and salt spray better than other warm-season grasses.

Different Selections

Several selections have been developed from the original strain of St. Augustine imported from the West Indies. The old selection, Bitterblue, and a dwarf selection, Seville, are often the top choice for partial shade, while other selections are not as shade tolerant. Floratine and dwarf selections such as Delmar, Jade, and Seville have narrower leaves, so they show unusually fine texture for St. Augustine. These fine-textured strains require careful, closer mowing to keep them looking good. All of the above selections are sometimes attacked by chinch bugs. Floratam II is resistant to the pests but has a coarser texture and is less shade tolerant than the other selections.

Raleigh, developed at North Carolina State University, is the most cold-tolerant selection and the best suited for planting in Zone 8

AT A GLANCE

❖

ST. AUGUSTINE
Stenotaphrum secundatum

Type: warm season
Green season: spring to fall
Dormant season: winter
Light: sun to partial shade
Soil: sandy, well drained
Water: medium to high
Planting method: sod, plugs, sprigs
Mowing height: 2½ to 4 inches
Range: Zones 8 to 10, warmer parts of Zone 7
Pests: chinch bugs, brown patch, gray leaf spot, mole crickets, SADV
Remarks: fast growing

and warmer sections of Zone 7. Raleigh also seems more tolerant of clay soils, while most other St. Augustine types prefer sandy soil. Delmar is a dwarf selection that shows some tolerance to cold, although not as much as Raleigh.

Planting and Care

St. Augustine is almost always planted from sod, plugs, or sprigs. Sprigs planted in late spring or early summer fill in quickly and usually form a solid turf within three months. You may be able to harvest your own sprigs by offering to edge the St. Augustine lawn of a friend or neighbor. A simpler way is to start with sod or plugs, which come in flats very similar to bedding transplants. See page 24 for more information about starting grasses from sod, sprigs, or plugs.

St. Augustine knits together to make a thick, wear-resistant turf.

You may see St. Augustine selections available from seed. These selections are very new and have yet to be proven, as St. Augustine typically produces little or no seed. If you are working with a large area and find seeding the only economical way to start, consider testing the seed in a small area first.

St. Augustine's need for fertilizer varies according to the soil's natural fertility and the amount of rainfall it receives. If your soil is very sandy and porous, fertilize St. Augustine in spring and once or twice each summer. Less fertilizer is needed on grass planted in heavier clay soils. Overfertilizing can make the grass produce so many stolons, or runners, that it becomes puffy with a thick layer of thatch. When this happens, dethatch the lawn with a power rake in early to midsummer. Limit fertilizer applications to a controlled-release product applied in spring when the grass begins to turn green, and again in late spring and summer.

Mow St. Augustine at a height of 3 to 4 inches to help the grass develop a deep root system. Dwarf selections such as Seville may be mowed at 2½ inches but will need a bit more water during periods of drought.

Troubleshooting

The chinch bug is a serious pest of St. Augustine lawns in many parts of the South. This insect devours the roots of the grass. Insecticides are available that can control this pest, but repeat applications are usually necessary. The St. Augustine selections Floralawn and Floratam are supposedly resistant to the pest, although strains of the insect which seem to feed on the grass have been found. West of the Mississippi River, a virus called St. Augustine Decline Virus (SADV) sometimes causes St. Augustine lawns to decline slowly. The only cure is to replant the area with a resistant strain (Floralawn, Floratam, or Seville) or to change to another lawn grass, such as Bermuda, centipede, or Zoysia, which is not susceptible to the virus.

Other problems include brown patch and a similar disease called take-all patch, gray leaf spot, and mole crickets. See pages 118–122 for more information about these pests and diseases.

Some selections of St. Augustine are tolerant of shade.

Zoysia

Zoysia is a stiff, fine-textured grass that makes a dense lawn.

Zoysia is the South's most refined warm-season grass. Fine, lush, and thick, it chokes out weeds and fills in bare spots. Zoysia tolerates drought, grows in sun or light shade, has few insect or disease problems, and becomes a smooth beige carpet in winter.

However, Zoysia is expensive to buy, and it is not the kind of grass you can neglect. But with proper care, a Zoysia lawn can look like green velvet.

In the Landscape

The dense texture of Zoysia makes it a pleasure to walk on. Its smooth surface also contrasts beautifully with other landscape features, and it is especially valuable in formal landscapes where every edge is manicured and every shrub is clipped. From a distance, it is difficult to distinguish a well-maintained Bermuda lawn from a lawn that is planted with Zoysia. Zoysia turns a lovely beige in winter, providing strong contrast when the lawn is framed with low evergreen shrubs or ground covers. Of all the warm-season grasses, Zoysia makes the nicest winter cover.

Zoysia spreads by rhizomes and stolons, but it grows slowly and is easy to keep out of nearby shrub beds and flowerbeds. It tolerates partial shade but will thin out in heavy shade.

Different Selections

Most Zoysia lawns are of the selections Meyer *(Zoysia japonica)* or Emerald *(Zoysia matrella)*. Meyer is not as fine textured nor as dark green as Emerald, but it is popular in the upper South because of its superior cold hardiness. Meyer is also a fast grower for a Zoysia grass. Sometimes called Z-52 Zoysia, Meyer tends to go dormant early in the fall and is slow to green up in spring.

Emerald is less cold hardy than Meyer but has a fine, dense texture and a very dark green color. Emerald is more shade tolerant than Meyer but may be damaged by winter temperatures in the upper South.

Choose one selection rather than mixing the two. Since Meyer and Emerald have slightly different textures and become dormant at varying times, mixing them can create a patchwork effect.

AT A GLANCE

❖

ZOYSIA

Zoysia japonica
Zoysia matrella

Type: warm season

Green season: spring to fall

Dormant season: winter

Light: sun to partial shade

Soil: fertile, well drained

Water: medium

Planting method: sod, sprigs, plugs

Mowing height: 1 to 2 inches

Range: Zones 6 to 8

Pests: dollar spot

Remarks: very dense, weed resistant

Planting and Care

The best time to plant Zoysia is early summer. You can plant it later in the season provided you give it plenty of water to encourage fast growth. Zoysia may be planted from sod, sprigs, or plugs. If you start with sprigs, it will take two years for the grass to grow together into a smooth lawn. Zoysia sod is ready for use as a lawn within weeks after planting.

Zoysia requires a good foundation of topsoil at least 6 inches deep. Cultivate and grade the soil carefully before laying sod; bumps and hills will make it impossible to mow the lawn smoothly. For best results, slope the soil very gently so that it will drain well. Zoysia cannot stand wet feet.

Zoysia grows slowly and uniformly, rarely looking unkempt even when it needs mowing.

How you mow Zoysia depends on the texture you would like to achieve. If you want a smooth, velvety finish, invest in a reel mower. Reel mowers cut lower and more cleanly than rotary mowers. Most people who want a highly refined Zoysia lawn also like to edge it with a nylon-string trimmer after each mowing. You can mow Zoysia at a height of 1 to 2 inches. The taller height will be more deeply rooted and easier to maintain.

Dry weather seldom kills Zoysia lawns, but it can weaken the turf and make it appear dormant in the middle of summer. To keep your Zoysia green through droughts, provide 1 inch of water weekly.

Weeds are seldom a problem in a well-maintained Zoysia lawn, for the dense growth naturally chokes out weeds. However, winter weeds such as wild onion are unsightly and difficult to control. For best results, dig them out by hand or spray with an approved weedkiller each time the weeds reappear. Patch the damaged area in spring when the Zoysia begins to turn green. See page 125 for more information about wild onion.

Zoysia prefers a soil pH between 6.0 and 6.5. Fertilize twice a year, just after the grass turns green in spring and late summer, using a balanced controlled-release fertilizer with iron such as 27-3-6.

Troubleshooting

Problems with insects, diseases, and weeds can often be traced to too much thatch. To check thatch in Zoysia, use a sharp knife to cut out a 2-inch plug in fall, just after the grass becomes dormant. If you see more than a ¾-inch-thick layer of thatch above the soil line, plan to dethatch your lawn next spring using a power rake.

If less thatch is present, you may be able to prevent further buildup by cutting the lawn very close in spring, just as the grass begins to turn green, and raking up all the material collected. Correcting the soil pH or top-dressing with a 1-inch layer of compost will stimulate the activity of soil microorganisms that break down dead stems and old clippings. It also helps limit the accumulation of thatch. Unless you are seriously overfertilizing your Zoysia, you should not need to dethatch more than once every three years. Some Zoysia lawns never need dethatching, but they should still be checked every fall for possible thatch problems.

Zoysia may be bothered by a fungal disease known as dollar spot. See page 119 for more information about this disease.

This Emerald Zoysia lawn is kept closely clipped like a putting green.

Ground Cover Profiles

Ground covers are the answer for trouble spots that are too shady, dry, or sloping for other plants. Their beauty and durability depend on the selection of the right ground cover for the site, as well as proper care and maintenance tailored to the species. Repeating or flowing ground cover plantings will help to unify your landscape. Once established, they also will provide valuable color and texture, yet require very little maintenance. They frame other landscape features and give your front yard and private outdoor living areas a refined, well-dressed appearance.

The ground covers described in the following pages were selected by the garden editors at *Southern Living* for their dependability and beauty in the garden. These are the most popular and reliable evergreen ground covers for home landscapes. You will find most of these ground covers for sale at garden centers, but you may need to purchase some of the more unusual selections through mail-order nurseries.

Arranged alphabetically by common name, these profiles include a description of each ground cover, details about planting and care, and ways that you can best use each ground cover in your landscape. Critical to your success with any ground cover that you have chosen is knowing where it grows best and the type of soil and sunlight it needs. This information, as well as possible problems and their solutions, is included in the profiles.

For a quick summary of each ground cover, refer to the *At a Glance* box that accompanies every profile. This box will give you the major features of the plant, including the type of light and soil the ground cover requires and how much water it prefers. Within each profile you will learn how each ground cover is usually planted and the best ways to keep the plants looking handsome during every season of the year. Names of popular species or selections are also listed in the profiles.

Ground covers, such as this mondo grass, offer variety and an alternative to lawn grasses.

Ajuga

The variegated foliage of Burgundy Glow ajuga contrasts with a darker-colored selection.

Several handsome plants grow in the shade, but most offer little color besides shades of green. Ajuga, also known as carpet bugleweed, comes to the rescue with colorful bronze, purple, green, or silvery pink variegated foliage and surprising spikes of blue or white flowers in the spring. Although it is sometimes short-lived, ajuga is a ground cover that is worth planting.

In the Landscape

Ajuga is ideal for partial sun to shade in the upper and middle South. In the lower South, plant ajuga where it will get shade during the hottest part of the day. Tough and vigorous, ajuga works best in places you want to cover with a solid carpet, such as in broad borders along walkways, beneath small trees, or in other locations where it will not crowd out less hardy plants. Ajuga also spreads among rocks on shady slopes and is a good ground cover to plant around raised stepping-stones. While ajuga grown in good conditions will make a dense, solid mass rapidly, after a period of time it may thin out or even die back. Therefore, it is best to use ajuga as a ground cover in areas that may be easily replanted, if needed, and are not likely to erode if the planting thins out or dies back.

Species and Selections

The most common type of ajuga is *Ajuga reptans* Rubra which has bronzish purple foliage and violet flower spikes that appear in early spring. You have a wide choice of ajuga selections, including Bronze Beauty (dark purple foliage), Burgundy Glow (burgundy, white, and green foliage), Alba (white flowers), and Variegata (pale green and white foliage). Burgundy Glow may take on the characteristics of its parent form, called Atropurpurea, which has darker leaves and is so vigorous that it can quickly take over a bed. To maintain a bed of any variegated ajuga, pull out some of the plants with very dark leaves in spring and fall to keep them from crowding out the others. The intensity of the coloration of the foliage has to do with the amount of sun the plant receives. While none of the types are exceptional in full sun, the foliage colors tend to be muted in deep shade.

A taller bugleweed, *Ajuga pyramidalis,* is popular for confined areas since it does not spread as fast as *Ajuga reptans.* It has green foliage and blue flowers and grows a bit taller. The selection called Metallica Crispa is very different, with small crinkled purplish leaves that have a metallic sheen.

Another species, *Ajuga genevensis,* sports all green leaves. Gardeners like it because it does not spread as fast as *Ajuga reptans,* which can spread out of bounds in a small area. It has 2-inch-tall blue flower spikes in spring. Unlike other ajugas, which are hardy to Zone 3, Geneva is hardy only to Zone 5.

Planting and Care

Clumps of *Ajuga reptans* spread rapidly when given rich, well-drained soil. New plants form at the tips of stolons, which the largest plants send out in all directions. Although the plants you buy in 4-inch pots are sold as singles, each pot may contain several plants. Carefully cut these apart with a sharp knife, and plant them right away. If you set them out in spring and water occasionally to promote steady growth, plants spaced 8 inches apart should grow together within a year.

Once ajuga is established, the plants can be divided as often as every season if the planting has grown thick enough to afford giving up a few plants. To propagate ajuga, simply dig up a healthy young crown with some roots attached, replant it in a new spot, and water well. In the coastal, lower, and middle South, early summer and early fall are the best times to propagate ajuga, but you can do it at any time of year, provided you keep the transplanted crowns watered and protect them from extreme cold or heat. In the upper South, plant or propagate in early spring.

Once ajuga is established, very few weeds are able to penetrate it, for the plants completely cover the soil with their spoon-shaped leaves that shade out most weeds. Maintenance is usually limited to trimming off the old flower spikes in late spring (if you find them unsightly) to keep the bed looking neat and to pulling up plants that try to grow where they are not wanted. Avoid fertilizing ajuga during warm, humid weather. If you think fertilizer is needed, apply it only in early spring or fall, using a controlled-release product such as 12-6-6.

Troubleshooting

Over time, large patches of ajuga may collapse and shrivel because of crown rot, a fungus that is worst during a period of hot, humid weather. If the fungus occurs, try trimming the infected leaves and top-dressing the area with 1 inch of compost. See page 119 for more information about crown rot.

A spread of ajuga in full bloom will bring a sweep of color to your garden in early spring.

Ardisia, Japanese

The crinkled texture of Japanese ardisia foliage contrasts handsomely with adjacent plants.

Many ground covers have trouble standing up to the humid heat of the Gulf Coast but not Japanese ardisia. This lush plant is perfect for carpeting the ground beneath trees or for filling small spaces where houses cast their shade. Increasingly popular in the lower South, Japanese ardisia features attractive evergreen foliage, copper-colored new growth, small white flowers in summer, and bright red berries in fall that last until they are eaten by birds and squirrels. While it is not winter hardy in the middle or upper South, in the lower and coastal South, Japanese ardisia is used in much the same way as Japanese pachysandra is used in cooler climates—as a low-maintenance ground cover in shady areas where lawn grasses will not grow.

In the Landscape

Japanese ardisia spreads by underground rhizomes, from which sprout short upright branches topped with rosettes of long, leathery evergreen leaves. Ardisia can be grown beneath trees that drop their leaves in the fall; in fact, the fallen leaves that filter through the foliage become a natural mulch. This ground cover is also at home in woodland gardens, where its slightly dimpled leaves provide striking contrast to the glossy foliage of magnolias and large evergreen shrubs. In small city yards where foot traffic is limited to broad walkways, Japanese ardisia serves quite well as an alternative to a lawn.

Ardisia does require shade, for too much sun can cause the leaves to turn yellow in late summer. Because of its spreading habit, ardisia is a good choice for sites where you need a ground cover to blanket a shady slope. It is especially popular in northeastern Florida and along the southeastern coast.

Different Selections

Most large plantings of Japanese ardisia have light green leaves that become darker green in winter. Variegated selections have been developed, including several with leaf margins edged in creamy white. These ardisias are more easily damaged by sun than selections with green foliage. They also grow more slowly. Gulf Green, Ito Fukurin, and White Caps are representative of this group.

A much more vigorous selection is called Red Tide. Different from other Japanese ardisias, Red Tide has long, narrow leaves with orange-red markings near their central veins and eye-catching red stalks.

AT A GLANCE
❖
JAPANESE ARDISIA
Ardisia japonica

Features: leathery foliage, summer flowers, fall berries

Colors: white flowers, red berries

Height: 1 foot

Light: partial to full shade

Soil: fertile, well drained, acidic, loose

Water: medium

Range: Zones 8 to 10

Pests: none specific

Remarks: stands up to heat and humidity

Planting and Care

Japanese ardisia needs loose, fertile soil that is well drained. Although it does grow well in areas that receive heavy rainfall, ardisia must not be forced to endure prolonged wet conditions. Prepare the site by removing weeds and grasses and enriching the soil with a 2-inch layer of peat moss or other organic matter.

Most plants available in nurseries are growing in 4-inch pots to 1-gallon containers. Look for plants with two or three stalks arising from the crown. When planted 12 inches apart in spring, these plants will first establish themselves and then send out spreading rhizomes late in their first summer. To help the plants spread, be sure to mulch the new planting with a 3-inch layer of finely ground pine bark or compost. By the next year the planting will grow together and start producing flowers and berries. The flowers are not particularly showy, and most of the berries are hidden by the foliage. However, birds and other wildlife have no trouble finding the berries, which they may carry to other parts of your yard. Occasionally, you may need to pull up seedlings that appear where you don't want them to grow.

If fertilized once a year in late winter or early spring, ardisia will show better color and grow more vigorously. For best results, scatter a balanced controlled-release fertilizer on the ground just before a rain.

Unusually cold winter weather can cause ardisia leaves to burn and brown. If this occurs, set your lawnmower at its highest setting and cut off the damaged leaves and stems before new growth appears in spring. You can also use pruning shears or a string trimmer to groom a bed of ardisia in late winter or early spring.

Japanese ardisia is a durable evergreen ground cover with graceful foliage similar to that of pachysandra.

83

Aspidistra

Aspidistra has very large leaves that give it a tropical look.

The large, dark green leaves of aspidistra contrast beautifully with smaller plants and are at their best when used as a dark backdrop for ferns or beds of colorful impatiens. This ground cover is seldom grown north of Atlanta, Georgia, and Dallas, Texas, for it rarely survives temperatures that cause its roots to freeze. However, along the Gulf Coast and in the lower South, aspidistra is unsurpassed as a bold accent for deeply shaded areas where few other plants will grow. Aspidistra is also known as cast-iron plant because it makes a nearly indestructible houseplant.

In the Landscape

Tremendously tolerant of shade, aspidistra thrives under wide roof overhangs, around the edges of shady decks, under magnolia trees, and against walls that are shaded during most of the day. It is often used as a ground cover around the bases of large trees, where it contrasts nicely with the color and craggy texture of tree bark. Although the soil beneath large trees tends to dry out quickly, aspidistra adapts well to dry soil and shade, provided it is occasionally drenched by heavy rains. Aspidistra can tolerate dry and dusty conditions, but it does best when the foliage is washed with normal rainfall and has adequate moisture. This tropical-looking ground cover complements

AT A GLANCE

❖

ASPIDISTRA
Aspidistra elatior

Features: broad, upright leaves
Colors: dark green leaves
Height: leaves 2 to 3 feet
Light: partial to deep shade
Soil: rich, well drained
Water: low to medium
Range: Zones 8 to 10
Pests: none specific
Remarks: will burn in the sun

ferns, palms, and other plants that look as though they may have been transplanted from a rain forest. In winter, aspidistra's evergreen leaves keep their good looks if sheltered from cold winter winds.

Different Selections

Most gardeners who have aspidistra probably obtained their first plants from other gardeners, for this ground cover has often been shared among friends and neighbors. At nurseries it is usually sold by its species name or as cast-iron plant. A shorter-growing variegated type with creamy spots called Milky Way is also available. Variegata, a variegated selection with white stripes, can be somewhat unpredictable; when it is grown in rich soil with good light, the white leaf stripes tend to fade.

Planting and Care

Aspidistra grows from thick, knobby roots that look somewhat like iris rhizomes. It is not a fast spreader, so you will need a number of plants to cover a large area quickly. Set the plants 6 inches apart in soil that has been amended with compost, leaf mold, or other organic matter. Barely cover the roots with soil, and keep them constantly moist for two weeks after planting. Late spring to early summer is the best planting time, but you can also plant aspidistra in early fall. It takes one to two years for new plantings to grow into robust clumps.

Severe winter weather often injures aspidistra leaves, and occasionally they may turn yellow and then brown by winter's end. Leave them intact until spring, for the withered leaves help protect the roots from cold. However, as soon as you see the first furled shoots emerging from the ground in March or April, use scissors or sharp pruning shears to clip the old leaves close to the ground. You can also cut individual leaves at any time during the warm months, just as you would if you were growing aspidistra indoors as a houseplant. If the leaves become dusty and unkempt looking, wash them by hosing them down or sprinkling once or twice a year, especially after the pollen season.

Aspidistra grows in clumps that will slowly spread to cover the surrounding area.

Cotoneaster, Bearberry

Bearberry cotoneaster is bright with orange-red berries in fall.

AT A GLANCE

❖

BEARBERRY COTONEASTER

Cotoneaster dammeri

Features: lustrous leaves, bright red berries

Colors: green to reddish leaves, white flowers

Height: 1 to 2 feet

Light: full sun to partial shade

Soil: well drained

Water: low

Range: Zones 4 to 7

Pests: aphids, fire blight, lacebugs, mealybugs

Remarks: good for sunny slopes

The cotoneaster family includes many species that grow into stiff shrubs, but the cotoneasters grown as ground covers spread horizontally, with branches sometimes growing 10 feet long. The woody stems of these ground cover shrubs can develop roots where they touch the soil, so they work well on slopes that are subject to erosion. Ground cover cotoneasters are often called bearberry cotoneasters. They grow best in the middle and upper South. In the lower South, they may not develop many bright berries in the fall and are often plagued by insects and diseases, especially fire blight.

In the Landscape

The weeping branches of cotoneaster look best when they cascade down a slope. Full sun to partial shade is preferred, and excellent drainage is a must. Cotoneaster's stiff, elegant branches produce tiny white flowers in spring, followed by bright red berries in the fall. Birds eventually gather up the berries, but fortunately the seeds do not germinate easily, so you will not be faced with unwanted plants sprouting unexpectedly in odd places.

These prostrate cotoneasters look best unpruned. Plant them where they can have plenty of room; do not plant cotoneasters near walkways or driveways where you would need to trim back the woody stems, for pruned branches tend to look rough. Cotoneasters are an excellent choice to plant near the top of sunbaked slopes that are held in place with rock or stone. They are also a good filler in a seldom-visited sunny spot where you would rather have a ground cover than an oversized swath of lawn.

Species and Selections

The selection named Coral Beauty is popular for its small leaves, green above and whitish underneath, which become especially showy when the plants are laden with bright orange-red berries. Coral Beauty is reliably evergreen throughout the South, though it may occasionally drop its leaves after extremely cold winters. Lowfast forms a dense, evergreen ground cover that hugs the ground and reaches no more than 1 foot in height. The Repandens selection of a slightly different species, *Cotoneaster salicifolius,* produces reddish leaves and bright red berries and is evergreen only in the middle South. Several other cotoneasters that show a creeping or spreading habit are widely available, but avoid any that are deciduous; when used as ground covers, these may be invaded by winter weeds.

Planting and Care

Cotoneasters are normally sold in 1- and 3-gallon containers, though you may find plants in smaller pots. If planted in spring about 4 feet apart, plants can be expected to spread 2 feet their first year and fill in the space completely the following summer. Meanwhile, you can prevent weed problems by mulching between plants with a landscape fabric or roll-out paper mulch topped with shredded bark or pine straw. After the first year, branches can take root through the paper mulch.

Water young cotoneaster plants in dry weather during their first two summers. Once established, cotoneasters are quite drought tolerant. When planted where they can spread freely in all directions, they almost never require pruning or trimming. Fertilize established plants once a year, in spring. In early summer, pull or cut out any weeds or woody seedlings that have invaded the planting.

Troubleshooting

The bacterial disease called fire blight, best known as a problem of pyracantha and apple and pear trees, occasionally infects cotoneasters. Affected stems appear black and shriveled. Cut them a few inches below the damaged section of stem, using pruning shears dipped in a solution of ¼ cup bleach per gallon of water. Promptly dispose of the pruned stems. Use a fire blight spray in early spring to help prevent reoccurrence. Sometimes mealybugs colonize cotoneaster; you can identify them as small, white, cottonlike masses on the stems.

Aphids, which are tiny pear-shaped insects, often attack the new growth in spring, sucking sap from the tender branches. Lacebugs will feed on the leaves in late spring and summer, leaving telltale black dots on the underside of the leaves. Control these insects by spraying with an approved insecticide.

The low, spreading branches of bearberry cotoneaster weave together and often root where they touch the ground.

Dianthus

The pink blossoms of Bath's Pink are delightfully fragrant.

AT A GLANCE

❖

DIANTHUS
Dianthus gratianopolitanus
Dianthus plumarius

Features: flowing foliage,
    fragrant flowers
Colors: gray-green leaves,
    magenta, pink, and red flowers
Height: 3 to 4 inches, 8 to 12
    inches in bloom
Light: full sun to partial shade
Soil: well drained
Water: medium
Range: Zones 3 to 9
Pests: none specific
Remarks: makes a dense carpet

Fragrant and featuring dusty gray foliage, dianthus has much to recommend it as a ground cover. The selections grown as ground covers are related to their more famous cousin, the carnation. But unlike carnations, which grow into upright plants, ground cover dianthus spreads into a solid mat of foliage. However, the carnation family similarities are evident in the flowers, which have a sweet, spicy fragrance and petals that look as though they have been trimmed with pinking shears. Cold winters seem to bring out the best in these plants, making them most adaptable to the middle and upper South.

In the Landscape

Although there are more than 200 types of dianthus, including annuals, biennials, and hardy perennials, only two species, *Dianthus gratianopolitanus* and *Dianthus plumarius,* are really useful as ground covers. *Dianthus gratianopolitanus* is often called Cheddar pinks, while *Dianthus plumarius* goes by the common name cottage pinks. These plants produce a dense, grassy gray-green cover that persists year-round. In spring, the silvery carpet becomes dotted with fragrant flowers on slender stems. Depending on the selection, the blossoms may be light pink, deep magenta, or some shade of pink in between.

The texture of dianthus is finer than that of most other ground covers. When it is planted in large areas, the foliage ripples over the ground, creating a soft, billowy look. Dianthus works well with many other plants and is especially striking near dwarf nandinas and large ornamental grasses.

This ground cover needs full sun but will tolerate partial afternoon shade. More than anything else, dianthus needs excellent drainage so that the roots never have to endure prolonged periods with soggy feet. Its neat growth habit and fine texture make it a perfect edging for concrete surfaces such as walkways and areas around swimming pools. Dianthus also looks good planted along the edge of a street, where it can spill gracefully over concrete curbs.

Species and Selections

The most popular ground cover dianthus for Southern gardens is a selection called Bath's Pink, which produces soft pink flowers that are wonderfully fragrant and are quite long-lived in cut arrangements. Other Cheddar pinks include Tiny Rubies, which produces rosy pink blossoms, and Petite, which has light pink blossoms; its foliage grows only 3 inches tall. Some selections offer slight variations in foliage color, including stronger blue-greens and clearer grays. Popular cottage pinks include Inchmery, which produces pale pink flowers, and Excelsior, which has a bright red blossom.

Planting and Care

The best ground cover dianthus are propagated by division rather than by seed, so you will need to start with purchased plants. Or you can dig divisions from the edges of established plantings in either spring or fall and transplant them to your garden. Use a sharp knife to cut tight clumps into plugs (with roots) about 1½ inches in diameter. Set plants or plugs 6 to 8 inches apart, and weed them regularly by hand until they grow together into a thick blanket.

Cheddar pinks can adapt to either sandy or clay soil, provided the site is sunny and well drained. Amend the soil with organic matter, such as compost, to improve its texture and drainage. If a soil test indicates that the soil is acidic, add lime or bone meal to raise the pH to between 6.5 and 7.0.

After the plants flower in spring, use scissors or pruning shears to cut the flowering stems even with the height of the foliage. Grooming the ground cover will keep it looking like a plush carpet. Because Cheddar pinks need good light and air circulation, remove any leaves or pine straw that fall on the plants in late fall. The foliage is too delicate and tangled to clean with a rake, but you may be able to gently sweep off dry fallen leaves or blow them off with a leaf blower.

An evergreen perennial, Cheddar pinks grow into a tightly knit mat of striking gray leaves.

Fern

Autumn fern has glossy, evergreen foliage that remains handsome through all seasons.

If you have a shady spot in your yard, you should grow ferns. No other family of plants offers such beautiful foliage and such a variety of patterns and sizes for so little care. Masses of ferns can serve as ground covers, or you can collect different hardy species to create a fern garden that becomes a tapestry of elegant foliage from spring until fall. Ferns that grow well in the South include both evergreen forms and deciduous types, which die back to their roots in the winter. Evergreen ferns are the most useful in places where you want a year-round ground cover.

In the Landscape

Most ferns need protection from hot afternoon sun, but you do not have to relegate them to a dark corner. In fact, many thrive in high shade or even dappled sun. Some tolerate drought, but almost all do better with consistent moisture.

The biggest reward for using ferns in the garden comes from combining them with other plants. They mix equally well with annuals, perennials, bulbs, and shrubs. Try contrasting their fine foliage with the coarser, bolder leaves of plants such as hosta, hydrangea, or Japanese fatsia. Or use them as a background for the bright red, pink, or white leaves of caladiums. Another possibility is to blend ferns with native plants, such as blue phlox, columbine, and mayapple.

When using ferns as ground covers, plant them in mass to create a foliage garden devoted to shades of green. Ferns are also a natural choice for planting next to a pond, a stream, or a water garden.

Species and Selections

In all parts of the South, you can easily find a good evergreen fern to serve as a ground cover, or you can use ferns as anchor plants in a fern garden. It is a good idea to try various species in your yard before investing in a large number of plants to use as a ground cover. You want to be sure that they will thrive in your area and continue to look good through winter. Look for ferns that are commonly grown in your area. The species discussed here are the most dependable evergreen ferns for Southern gardens.

Autumn Fern

In the middle and upper South, autumn fern *(Dryopteris erythrosora)* is a good choice for shady locations or in the dappled light under pines. This native of China and Japan offers unusual variations in

In early spring, the new fronds of Christmas fern stand nearly straight. Later, they relax.

foliage color. The young fronds that emerge from the plants' centers are bronze and turn light green after a few weeks. Autumn fern eventually grows to nearly 2 feet tall. This fern can tolerate dry conditions for short periods of time but produces new fronds faster when it is grown in moist soil. Autumn fern is one of the hardiest of all evergreen ferns. In two years' time, healthy plants set 14 inches apart will gradually spread to fill in the space between them. In winter, these ferns remain upright in the garden, creating a surprisingly lush winter look.

Christmas Fern

Christmas fern *(Polystichum acrostichoides)* is native to the moist woodlands of the eastern United States. This fern was often used in Colonial times as cut material for holiday decorations—hence its name. Christmas fern has large, leathery leaves that grow 1 to 2 feet tall; in winter, these fronds tend to lie close to the ground. In the wild, Christmas fern is usually found growing on shady northern slopes near streams and rivers. Provide this type of exposure to ferns in your garden, and the plant is certain to survive. To create a ground cover with Christmas fern, set plants 12 inches apart, and trim some of the fronds after transplanting. The best times to move or plant Christmas ferns are spring or early fall.

AT A GLANCE
❖
CHRISTMAS FERN
Polystichum acrostichoides

Features: evergreen foliage
Colors: green
Height: 1 to 2 feet
Light: shade or filtered sun
Soil: moist, rich
Water: medium to high
Range: Zones 3 to 9
Pests: none specific
Remarks: fronds cascade downward when fern is grown on slopes

Holly fern has the height and permanence of a low shrub but is much looser than most shrubs.

AT A GLANCE
❖
HOLLY FERN
Cyrtomium falcatum

Features: glossy foliage
Colors: dark green
Height: 2 to 3 feet
Light: partial shade or filtered sun
Soil: moist, rich
Water: medium
Range: Zones 8 to 10
Pests: none specific
Remarks: tolerates some sun and dry soil

Holly Fern

A robust, dark green fern that looks almost like a shrub, holly fern *(Cyrtomium falcatum)* is the perfect choice for open wooded areas in the middle and lower South. This fern can take more sun and dryness than other ferns. The shiny, toothed leaves look somewhat like holly foliage. Plants grow 2 to 3 feet tall and spread slowly; they do best when planted quite shallow, with a loose mulch to protect the roots. Holly fern is usually not evergreen in areas where temperatures fall consistently below 20 to 25 degrees. In cold winter areas, you can keep the plants in large pots, which are buried to their rims in the garden in summer, and bring the pots indoors during the winter.

Shield Fern

Also known as wood ferns, shield ferns have fronds that are shaped like long triangles, broader at the base than they are at their pointed tips. Several species of shield fern are native to the South and others come from Asia. Shield ferns are not reliably evergreen, but any Southern gardener can find a type of shield fern that will serve well as a semievergreen ground cover.

The hardiest evergreen shield fern, often called Goldie's Woodfern or Goldie's fern, grows wild in the northern Appalachians. Classified as *Dryopteris goldiana*, this is the most vigorous of the wood ferns that grow as a ground cover in the upper South. Plant this large fern, which can grow 3 feet tall, in a place that gets open shade and plenty of moisture. Shaggy shield fern *(Dryopteris atrata)*, a smaller, 1-foot-tall shield fern from Asia, is a good ground cover to grow around the bases of large trees in a woodland garden. A third shield fern that is hardy in the middle and upper South is the marginal shield fern *(Dryopteris marginalis)*. This rather upright fern grows to 2 feet tall and has very lacy, finely cut foliage. Marginal shield fern strongly prefers moist, cool shade and is best grown in shady mountain landscapes in the upper South.

In the lower South, the shield fern of choice is *Dryopteris ludoviciana,* or Florida shield fern. This fern is native to the swamps and lowlands of the deep South and is very easy to grow. Southern shield fern *(Thelypteris kunthii)* thrives in hot, humid weather and grows well in many conditions, from partial sun to deep shade. It can grow as tall as 4 feet and is an enthusiastic spreader. Start new plantings by setting plants 18 inches apart. Although this fern is evergreen, in very cold years it may lose many of its fronds in winter.

You may choose from different types of shield ferns, or wood ferns, to serve as a ground cover in your landscape.

Trim the dead fronds to make the planting look neat and to make way for new fronds, which will begin to unfurl in early spring. It will grow in the middle South but will lose its evergreen quality and die back to the ground each winter.

Planting and Care

The ferns discussed here require moist, rich soil. The soil pH should be acidic to near neutral but never alkaline. To assure the right root environment for ferns, dig planting holes and enrich them with sphagnum compost, leaf mold, and peat moss. Before setting out container-grown plants, trim off some of the older fronds and the fronds that are broken or have become damaged. Water well, and keep the newly planted ferns constantly moist for at least two weeks. Until they are well established, even the most drought-tolerant ferns benefit from regular watering.

Ferns develop new fronds year-round, though most of the new growth takes place in spring and early summer. Fertilizer is not always needed but can help improve the foliage color of some species. To fertilize ferns, use a controlled-release fertilizer that releases its nutrients slowly so that it will not burn the plants' sensitive shallow roots.

Frequently, the tips of fronds darken and shrivel after they have released spores. Old fronds also die off naturally as new ones grow from the plants' centers. When old fronds wither, you can snip them off to keep the planting looking neat, but this grooming is not required. Few insects and diseases bother ferns.

AT A GLANCE
❖
SHIELD FERN
Dryopteris species

Features: broad, finely cut foliage

Colors: medium green

Height: 2 to 4 feet

Light: shade or filtered sun

Soil: moist, rich

Water: medium to high

Range: Zones 6 to 9

Pests: none specific

Remarks: rugged ferns for woodland gardens

Hellebore

Lenten rose, the most durable of the hellebores, produces late-winter blooms that linger into spring.

AT A GLANCE
❖
HELLEBORE
Helleborus species

Features: glossy leaves, winter flowers

Colors: green foliage, rose, cream, green, or white blossoms

Height: 8 to 14 inches

Light: shade

Soil: fertile, moist, well drained

Water: medium

Range: Zones 4 to 8

Pests: none specific

Remarks: long-lived evergreen ground cover for shady areas

Two characteristics make hellebores valuable ground cover plants in Southern gardens: they thrive in deep shade, and they flower beginning in late winter, when few other ground covers have blossoms. Hellebores can be grown as perennials or as ground covers. Individual plants do not creep and spread like other ground covers but shed seeds that grow into new seedlings to create a colony. The large, leathery leaves look like fans on upright stalks and remain evergreen all winter. In January through April, they are joined by nodding flowers. The flowers last weeks in the garden although they become paler in time.

In the Landscape

Raised beds around the bases of trees are ideal spots for hellebores, which require full summer shade and partial winter sun. Hellebores bloom in late winter. Because the cup-shaped flowers nod downward toward the ground, placing them where they are slightly raised makes them easier to enjoy up close. This ground cover is ideal to interplant with ferns or caladiums, or it may be grown in woodland gardens beneath forsythias, rhododendrons, and other shrubs that have sparse, spreading branches. When exposed to too much summer sun, the stalks may lie flat on the ground and die out. New leaves appear when temperatures cool in the fall.

Species and Selections

Four hellebore species are commonly grown in shady Southern gardens. The most popular one is known as Lenten rose *(Helleborus orientalis)*. As the easiest hellebore to grow, it is perhaps the preferred species for use as a ground cover. Flowers appear from January through April in shades of cream to burgundy and are sometimes marked with purple.

Christmas rose *(Helleborus niger)* blooms slightly later than Lenten rose and produces lovely white flowers. Christmas rose is somewhat challenging to grow and does best in the middle and upper South, where winters are cold. A more robust but harder to find species, bearsfoot hellebore *(Helleborus foetidus)* has large, leathery leaves and is slightly more tolerant of drought than the other species. Bearsfoot hellebore produces clusters of apple green flowers, often edged in purple, in January and February. Another hellebore that is difficult to find is green hellebore *(Helleborus viridis)*. It may die down during periods of drought and often cannot be counted on for year-round evergreen foliage.

Planting and Care

Hellebores grow best in rich, moist soil that is neutral or slightly alkaline. Work plenty of organic matter into the soil so that it will hold moisture. Also add a bit of sand to tight clay soil to improve its drainage. Unless your soil is naturally alkaline, add lime to bring the pH up to neutral, or about 7.0. Fall is the best time to plant new hellebores, though they may be set out in early spring. Set plants 12 inches apart, and mulch between the plants with shredded bark or another organic mulch.

New plants are often slow to become established, so be patient. Depending on their size and when they are planted, they may not bloom until their second or third winter in the ground. Once established, hellebores require very little care, and individual plants can live for many years. They prefer to grow undisturbed, but should you decide to dig up a seedling to move or share with a friend, take care not to mangle the roots of plants left behind.

Regular maintenance in the hellebore bed consists of checking the pH of the soil every fall to see whether additional lime is needed and trimming off leaves that become ragged and unsightly if scorched by cold winter winds. Fertilize lightly once a year, in fall, by sprinkling a low nitrogen (9-6-6) balanced controlled-release fertilizer around the plants. Then refresh the mulch with a light layer of new material. Water hellebores thoroughly with enough water to penetrate the soil deeply (1 inch) during periods of summer drought.

Because Lenten rose will seed itself, a planting grows larger with each year.

Ivy

Algerian ivy grows well in the warm, humid coastal South.

Although ivy is a clinging, climbing evergreen vine, some types, such as the well-known English ivy, are popular ground covers for low-maintenance beds. The cut stems of ivy also make fine filler material for flower arrangements. You can use small rooted pieces to add elegance and charm to pots and planters containing summer annuals.

Ivy has a reputation for getting out of hand. When trimmed and pruned periodically, however, ivy can easily be kept from crawling up trees and buildings. Ivy clings to support with suckerlike rootlets, which attach themselves to wood, brick, and other surfaces. As long as you cut back your ivy when it wanders beyond its intended space, it will always look neat and should not cause problems.

In the Landscape

Ivy is at its best when planted in mass in places that receive mostly shade in summer and filtered sun in winter. Its color and texture depends on the species and selection you choose, but all types of ivy appear lush and attractive during every season of the year.

Ivy is especially useful as a ground cover on banks that are prone to erosion or are awkward to mow. One way to keep the ivy from spreading is to design the planting so that it has definite edges that can be easily trimmed. Hard edges such as low walls or walkways or areas of regularly mowed lawn contrast beautifully with ivy's handsome texture and make edge maintenance easy. If you do not want ivy to spread into perennial beds or shrub borders or climb on buildings, avoid planting it next to them. You will need to trim ivy a couple of times during the growing season if it starts to climb up the trunks of trees.

As with many other evergreen ground covers, you can underplant ivy with daffodils, tulips, and other spring flowering bulbs.

Species and Selections

The most common form of ivy, called English ivy *(Hedera helix),* has small, glossy, dark green leaves and can form a dense ground cover up to 12 inches tall. Variegated forms, such as Glacier, are available. The white-edged leaves of these selections are especially attractive in small shady spots where they will be viewed up close. Other types of English ivy include Baltica, which has dark green leaves with prominent white leaf veins, and Needlepoint, which is sometimes called bird's foot ivy because of its long, pointed leaf lobes. In addition to these, there are over 100 types available that vary in leaf size and shape. Many sold as houseplants are hardy outdoors.

AT A GLANCE

❖

IVY
Hedera species

Features: lovely lobed leaves
Colors: green, variegated
Height: 6 to 12 inches
Light: partial sun to shade
Soil: well drained
Water: medium
Range: Zones 3 to 10
Pests: none specific
Remarks: requires regular trimming

A slightly different species called Algerian ivy *(Hedera canariensis)* is more popular in the warmest coastal areas of the South. The glossy leaves of Algerian ivy are usually larger than those of English ivy, up to 5 inches across, and the plants thrive on abundant moisture. In addition to the standard green form, a very showy white-edged version, Gloire-de-Marengo, makes a gorgeous ground cover on slopes that do not face to the south or west where they bake in the sun. Algerian ivy grows in Zones 8 to 10.

The somewhat uncommon Persian or colchis ivy *(Hedera colchica)* has large, dark green leaves with a leathery (rather than glossy) finish and slighted rounded (rather than pointed) leaf edges. Its growth habit is slower than that of English ivy, and Persian ivy is less tolerant of full sun. The variegated form, which has creamy white leaf edges, does especially well in shade. This ivy is generally used in small spaces as a ground cover. Large masses are not common.

Planting and Care

Adaptable and easy to grow, ivy thrives in almost any soil. Once established, ivy shades the ground so thoroughly that weeds are seldom a problem. However, you must watch new plantings closely for invading weeds; pull them out promptly.

You will get the fastest growth from well-rooted plants, which are usually sold in 2- or 4-inch pots. Prepare the soil by removing all weeds, and make holes for each plant 12 to 18 inches apart. On slopes, you might try using a landscape fabric to control weeds. Set the plants in holes cut in the material. Then cover the spaces between plants with a 3-inch-thick mulch of pine straw to maintain soil moisture and make the new planting look neat.

The ivy should fill in within two years. Once it is established, use a nylon-string trimmer or a sharp spade to trim around the edges of the planting every few weeks during the summer. Sometimes very old plantings become so thick that they cannot grow well. To restore the bed's beauty, set the lawnmower blade at its highest level, and mow over the planting in early spring, or use a nylon-string trimmer with a blade attachment to shear off all but the lowest 3 inches of growth. Rake off the debris, and fertilize with a controlled-release fertilizer just before a rain.

The only problem with ivy is that it is difficult to eradicate unless you spray with a nonselective herbicide such as Roundup. Use ivy only in the most permanent parts of your landscape.

English ivy makes a dense carpet of interwoven vines.

Juniper

Shore juniper forms a feathery, creeping cover ideal for sites with full sun and poor, sandy soil.

Sorting through junipers can be confusing, for there are hundreds of types including wide, upright, and columnar shrubs and creeping types used for ground cover. Some of the smaller upright types can serve as ground covers, but the term "ground cover juniper" is usually reserved for prostrate selections that grow less than 1 foot tall and spread horizontally. Like their taller relatives, ground cover junipers are extremely tough plants that can tolerate both hot sun and cold, drying winds. If you need a low-maintenance ground cover for an eroded slope or some other dry area with poor soil, you need look no further than these junipers.

In the Landscape

The water misers of the ground cover world, junipers are an excellent choice for slopes exposed to cold winter winds and hot summer sun. They are also ideal for dry, sandy soils where many other plants will not grow. Whether grown in troublesome spots or less stressful settings, junipers' fine texture and stiff, symmetrical growth complement many landscapes, especially business and commercial properties. These ground covers are especially attractive in designs where their blue-green or gray-green foliage contrasts with the darker-colored evergreens or with dormant winter lawns. Junipers are often used to stabilize banks, for their formal demeanor works well where you want simplicity. You can also use ground cover junipers near entryways or beneath small ornamental trees as long as there is plenty of sun. The greatest risk with junipers is planting too many of them, which can make your landscape appear boring or like a commercial landscape.

When choosing sites for junipers, be wary of areas in which there is too much shade or too much water. A little afternoon shade is fine, but all ground cover junipers basically thrive in full sun. If you have installed a lawn irrigation system, be sure to place these ground covers where they will not be reached by the spray, for too much moisture encourages root rot.

Species and Selections

There are more than a dozen ground cover junipers suitable for Southern gardens, and it is a good idea to seek the advice of a local nursery professional when choosing the best one for your yard. The following are probably the most common and versatile ground cover junipers. Creeping juniper, *Juniperus horizontalis,* is known for its mat of low, spreading, horizontal branches. It is ideal to use on gentle slopes or nearly flat areas, where it forms a lovely base for vertical accents that do not cast heavy shade, such as statuary, lampposts, or rock outcroppings. Blue Rug *(Juniperus horizontalis* Wiltonii) is the most popular selection. Its silvery steel blue foliage eventually spreads into a mat 8 feet across but only 3 to 6 inches tall. Andorra *(Juniperus horizontalis* Plumosa) is a selection known for its purplish bronze winter blush and the upright habit of the tips of its branches, which can reach 18 inches in height. Creeping junipers do best in the middle and upper South. Summer rain and humidity in the lower and coastal South cause stems to die and roots to rot.

The most heat-tolerant ground cover juniper, *Juniperus conferta,* is called shore juniper since it grows well in dry, sandy soils near the seashore where it will even tolerate salty ocean spray. This low-trailing juniper has bright green foliage, grows to a height of 8 to 12 inches, and is less stiff than other junipers. Shore juniper prefers thin, dry soil and is very popular in sandy, coastal regions. It is subject to root rot in heavy or wet soils. Plants spread to 8 feet across and sometimes produce black berries in the fall. Blue Pacific, one of the most popular selections, is named for its blue-green foliage. Silver Mist has silvery blue needles and a more compact form.

Parsons juniper *(Juniperus davurica* Expansa*)* is a widely grown selection that spreads up to 6 feet. It grows about 1 foot tall at first but eventually may stretch to 2 to 2½ feet in height.

For finely textured, feathery blue-green foliage, *Juniperus procumbens* Nana is a good choice. This juniper is generally referred

Parsons is one of the most popular juniper selections.

99

Andorra juniper is often chosen for its bronze winter color.

to as dwarf procumbens juniper or Japgarden juniper. Its branches radiate to a length of about 4 feet, sometimes developing supplemental roots along the ground, albeit slowly, as this juniper grows less vigorously than others. Several dwarf selections grow to a uniform height of only 6 to 8 inches. Where winters are very cold, the foliage may turn reddish in winter. Common selections include Greenmound and Variegata.

Planting and Care

Because ground cover junipers prefer soil that is not rich and fertile, no special soil preparation is needed beyond removing existing grasses and weeds and breaking up the heavy clay of compacted soil. Plants are usually sold in 1- or 2-gallon containers and may be planted at any time of the year. When planting junipers on slopes, you can get faster cover by planting them 2 to 3 feet apart at first. After two years, you may take out every other plant to give the remaining ones more room to grow. Or space plants 5 feet apart from the beginning, and keep some mulch between plants until they fill in the space. First mulch the planted slope with wheat or oat straw until the ground is barely covered. Then mulch over the straw with a 3-inch-layer of pine needles.

Like all other young plantings, junipers need water only if a severe drought develops after their first year in the ground. To bring out the best in the foliage color of junipers, avoid heavy fertilization unless they are growing in porous sand that lacks nutrients. Ground cover junipers require pruning only when they are damaged or diseased.

One of the greatest problems in beds of junipers is grass and grassy weeds, which will grow up through juniper foliage and are nearly impossible to pull. Be diligent about controlling weeds in beds for the first year or two or until the junipers grow into a cover thick enough to choke out weeds. Also, replenish mulch regularly to help minimize weeds.

Troubleshooting

Junipers are relatively pest free but can be devastated by mites if they should attack. The tiny, spiderlike mites are sheltered in the crevices between the needlelike juniper leaves. To control mites, you must use an approved systemic insecticide.

Root rot can be a problem in heavy clay. To avoid root rot, be sure the area has proper drainage.

Lamb's-ears

To understand how this plant got its name, all you have to do is touch a downy leaf. The leaves are so well clothed in soft hairs that they are almost furry, making them of great interest to children. They also bring interest to the garden, for their silvery gray color and glowing texture are unmatched by other plants. Most selections also develop flowering stalks studded with light purple flowers in early summer. These flower stalks are useful in flower arrangements and are very attractive to honeybees. But because they stretch up over the plant, they reduce the effects of the neat mat of silvery leaves.

Lamb's-ears is hardy in the South, though the plant will occasionally lose its leaves when badly bruised by accumulated ice in winter. New leaves will appear in spring. Hot, humid summer weather can cause problems, too, especially if the weather is so damp and humid that the hairy leaves rot because they never have a chance to dry.

In the Landscape

Lamb's-ears is a perennial that acts like a ground cover. Although the plants do form solid colonies that hug the ground, after a year or so the oldest stems tend to shed some leaves, which makes the planting look sparse in the middle. For this reason, lamb's-ears is best used in small places where it can be groomed easily or as a broad edging near walkways and driveways. At least a half day of sun is needed to keep the plant from drooping over too much. When the late afternoon sun lights up the plant's frosty-looking leaves, the effect is breathtaking.

Because of its luminous foliage, lamb's-ears is a perfect counterpoint to very brightly colored flowers and is a beautiful complement to flowering plants such as bearded iris. When planted in front of dark-colored evergreen shrubs, it creates a striking contrast. Yet another way to put lamb's-ears to work is to use ground cover plantings to visually unify landscapes that include other gray features, such as gray stonework or concrete. Lamb's-ears can repeat these hues but in a softer way.

Different Selections

Lamb's-ears is often shared among friends, for this ground cover is easily dug and divided. Nurseries do sell named selections, however. The best ground cover selection is Silver Carpet, which rarely blooms and therefore requires less maintenance than other selections. Countess Helen von Stein is also remarkable; its leaves are quite large, with serrated edges and distinct veins. In mail-order

Lamb's-ears is named for the shape and texture of its leaves.

AT A GLANCE
❖
LAMB'S-EARS
Stachys byzantina

Features: soft, fuzzy leaves
Colors: gray foliage, lavender
  flowers
Height: 6 to 12 inches
Light: full sun to partial shade
Soil: moist, well drained
Water: medium
Range: Zones 4 to 8
Pests: none specific
Remarks: light neutral color
  contrasts with darker plants

The gray, fuzzy leaves of lamb's-ears create a unique ground cover that is suitable for small areas where trimming can be done as needed during the year.

catalogs, the primary species of lamb's-ears, usually listed as *Stachys byzantina,* is sometimes given as *Stachys lanata* or *Stachys olympica.* A few selections produce white flowers, but the ones named here are the best for use as ground covers.

Planting and Care

Either potted plants or divisions taken from mature plants with a few roots attached may be planted in spring, early summer, or fall. Set them in moist, well-drained soil that barely covers the roots. Allow 10 inches between plants. Keep the plants moist until new growth appears, but avoid wetting the leaves late in the day. A light mulch of pine straw or finely shredded bark can suppress weeds and help retain soil moisture.

Plants usually become leggy after a year's growth, but each leggy stem develops roots where it touches the ground. You can renovate plantings without digging them up by cutting the plants back or by simply pulling out old crowns that have withered. Do this in late winter before new growth begins. There is no need to fertilize lamb's-ears, as it does fine in well-prepared garden soil.

Plants will need grooming, especially after they flower. Cut faded flower stalks with pruning shears. In spring, remove older, matted leaves to foster new growth.

Liriope

Liriope forms a blanket of clumping, grasslike plants.

The beauty of liriope, also known as big blue or monkey grass, is in its simplicity. Liriope's grasslike foliage grows thick and even, as if it has been groomed. Care free and dependable, liriope grows into a lush green carpet in shade or in sun, depending on the selection; then it blooms in spears of purple or white during the hottest weeks of summer. Evergreen except during the coldest winters, liriope is a dependable hardy perennial that tolerates drought and is not bothered by any serious pests.

In the Landscape

Liriope is often used to edge sidewalks, driveways, and shrub borders, but it is more than just a border grass. Planted in broad sweeps, liriope can be effective as a lawn substitute in difficult situations, such as beneath shallow-rooted trees or on shaded slopes. Another attribute is that it can add a different shade of green to the landscape. Choose one of the dark green forms or a bright, variegated type.

If, like many gardeners, you have a narrow band of liriope lining a walkway, consider digging up the border, dividing the plants into clumps of six to eight stems, and replanting them in a wide band on either side. This technique makes a narrow sidewalk seem wider and your entrance more gracious.

Liriope also can be used as a specimen plant in a container. Or choose a tall selection for an easy-care accent plant that tolerates drought and has no serious pests. You can plant liriope under trees and shrubs grown in containers or beneath young trees or shrubs that will eventually grow up and shade the bed. Or use it in mass to link several trees and shrubs together.

Species and Selections

There are many types of liriope that are nearly the same in form, yet vary in the width of their foliage and overall height. Mondo grass is a less cold-tolerant relative of liriope and is sometimes called dwarf lilyturf. Mondo grass has narrower leaves and a finer texture than liriope. (See the Mondo Grass profile on page 106.)

The most familiar form of liriope is big blue liriope *(Liriope muscari)*. The selection called Majestic has the showiest flowers, producing a spike that fans out at the top when it is fully mature.

AT A GLANCE
❖
LIRIOPE
Liriope muscari
Liriope spicata

Features: narrow, straplike leaves
Colors: lilac or white flowers
Height: 8 to 36 inches
Light: sun to full shade
Soil: fertile, well drained
Water: medium
Range: Zones 5 to 10
Pests: none specific
Remarks: low maintenance and adaptable to varied conditions

The flower spikes of liriope appear in late summer. Most selections produce purple flowers.

Silvery Sunproof is a variegated selection with light purple flowers. It is among the best for sunny spots.

There are several different selections that are variegated. They vary in size and degree of variegation, so it is important to select all of the same kind when planting in mass. Monroe White is noted for its white flowers but likes shade. Evergreen Giant is the tallest selection, reaching a height of 2 to 3 feet; however, it is dependably hardy only in Florida and South Texas. The other forms of liriope are winter hardy throughout the South but absolutely require shade in the hottest sections. In the southernmost regions of Texas and Florida, shade is needed to keep liriope's foliage from burning.

As its name implies, creeping liriope *(Liriope spicata)* differs from the big blue liriope in that it is a more vigorous spreader and generally has a narrower leaf (¼ inch wide) than big blue liriope, which has leaves from ⅜ to ¾ inches wide. While this spreading habit can be used to your advantage in a large bed, do not choose creeping liriope for a contained border. One popular variegated selection is Silver Dragon, which is the most sun tolerant of all.

Planting and Care

Whether you dig your starter plants from an established planting or purchase container-grown plants, you will need to divide the clumps. (By doing so, you will stretch your landscaping budget.) Plants more than five years old will be so thick that you will need a sharp knife or a hatchet to split the dense crown. Cut clumps into smaller clumps that have six to eight stems with roots attached. Discard rootless pieces that fall away as you divide the clumps. Divide clumps into single plantlets, if you have time, to get the most even, uniform stand.

Prepare the bed by tilling and mixing a 2-inch layer of organic matter such as compost, leaf mold, or peat moss into the soil. Rake the bed level, and apply a thick mulch before planting to keep down weeds and retain soil moisture. Then plant through the mulch.

Plant divisions 6 inches apart (12 inches for the tallest-growing types). Put them slightly deeper into the ground than the plants that were growing there previously to prevent them from washing out of the soil during a heavy rain. Keep your new bed or border evenly moist, and your liriope will have a firm hold in about 30 days. When planted in spring, it will multiply noticeably its first year and will fill in between plants by the end of its second summer. You can speed its spread by trimming the foliage back by half before planting. This encourages new growth.

Do not be alarmed if the foliage becomes brown and droopy after a severe winter. Just use your garden shears, a lawnmower set at the highest setting, or a nylon-string trimmer to clip the old leaves in late winter or early spring, before the new shoots begin to grow. When trimming, do not cut too close to the crown or you may destroy the coming season's earliest new growth. After trimming, feed liriope with a controlled-release fertilizer to encourage new growth.

After the flowers fade at summer's end, stalks of black berries will remain. You can remove these if they detract from the bed, but this can be quite a task for extensive plantings. The berries will disappear on their own in late fall or winter.

Evergreen Giant, the tallest selection of liriope, grows to the height of a small shrub (left side of the walkway). A variegated selection, which is more of a typical ground cover height (right side of walkway), will eventually form a solid cover.

Mondo Grass

When planted in mass, the dark green leaves of mondo grass appear soft and uniform.

Mondo grass is an ideal ground cover for shady spots in the warmer sections of the South. It succeeds under huge oaks and maples and in other shady areas where few plants will grow and remains a vibrant dark green all year long.

This ground cover has narrower leaves than the larger, more upright liriope, with which it is sometimes confused. (See the Liriope profile on page 103.) Mondo grass is less cold tolerant than liriope and cannot survive the cold winters of the upper South.

In the Landscape

Mondo grass can be used as a border grass along sidewalks and driveways, but it is at its best when used in a mass planting. Because of its fine texture, mondo grass, when planted in mass, creates a solid green mat with a windswept look. And if your house has windows near the ground, mondo grass is ideal as a foundation planting, especially on the shady side of the house.

One of the most popular uses for mondo grass is to group a number of plants in small shady spaces bordering walkways. Mulched with pine straw until the plants fill in, these islands of mondo grass require minimal maintenance, look much healthier than a shade-stressed lawn, and always appear neat and graceful. Some gardeners even use mondo grass as a substitute for a lawn, mowing it regularly to give it a more grasslike appearance.

Species and Selections

Mondo grass (*Ophiopogon japonicus*) can be distinguished from liriope by its modest 4- to 8-inch height and narrow individual leaves (only ⅛ inch wide). And while mondo grass does sometimes bear lilac or white flowers in spring, they usually go unnoticed as they are tiny and hidden by the foliage. Mondo grass spreads by underground stolons but rarely grows out of bounds. Dwarf mondo grass (*Ophiopogon japonicus* Nana) is an even shorter selection that grows in tiny tufts only 3 to 4 inches tall but spreads very slowly. There is also a purplish black species (*Ophiopogon planiscapus* Arabicus) that pairs well with the chartreuse and lighter-colored foliages of hosta.

Snakebeard (*Ophiopogon jaburan*) is a taller (18 inches), coarser-textured relative of mondo grass suitable for use in containers or as specimen plants in small spaces. The selection called Variegatus is particularly attractive with its coloration becoming a lighter yellow as it receives more sun.

AT A GLANCE
❖
MONDO GRASS
Ophiopogon species

Features: thin, grass-like leaves
Colors: dark green
Height: 3 to 18 inches
Light: shade
Soil: fertile, well drained
Water: medium
Range: Zones 7 to 10
Pests: none specific
Remarks: fine texture

Planting and Care

To create a mass planting of mondo grass, begin with purchased plants or clumps dug from an established stand. Keep the plants damp if you must wait for more than a day or so before planting.

Because mondo grass fills in more slowly than liriope, it is important to eradicate weeds and properly prepare the site before planting. If you attempt to grow mondo grass where common Bermuda has grown and where there is enough sun to promote Bermuda's vigorous growth, you must remove every sprig and rhizome of Bermuda. Otherwise, you will be fighting an endless battle with it as you attempt to grow a weedless swath of mondo grass. You may need to wait through the first half of the growing season to kill Bermuda grass as it reappears. Turn the soil once a month for several months so that all sprouts of Bermuda grass will grow up where you can kill them. Then plant the mondo grass.

Till or dig the soil 4 to 6 inches deep, and add plenty of organic matter, such as compost, leaf mold, or peat moss. Set out the small clumps in a gridlike pattern 6 inches apart. (See diagram on page 46.) This will make your planting look neat and orderly and will also allow your mondo grass to fill in evenly. Water young plantings during dry spells for the first year to help them fill in a little faster. During periods of extremely hot, dry weather, mondo grass may turn brown on the tips if not watered.

Normally, mondo grass does not need yearly grooming, but unusually severe winter weather can leave it looking a bit ragged by early spring. If your mondo grass is unsightly because of a bad winter, you can quickly restore its good looks. In late winter, set the blade of your lawnmower at its highest height, and attach the bagger if you have one. On a day when the mondo grass foliage is dry, mow over the bed. After mowing, rake the area with a leaf rake to remove any dead crowns as this will promote new growth. Then fertilize with a controlled-release fertilizer. Water the trimmed mondo grass if rain is not expected, and renew the mulch if the planting is young and has not yet filled in. By late spring, new foliage will appear to replace the leaves lost to winter weather.

The fine-textured foliage of mondo grass gives the effect of a lawn grass, especially if it is mowed.

Moss

Remove leaves and straw from mossy ground covers shortly after they fall.

Many Southern gardeners become frustrated when moss grows where they want to have grass. A good alternative is to cultivate your moss rather than try to get rid of it. Moss used as a ground cover in places where it naturally grows well produces a soft green glow that will convince you to consider planting this unconventional ground cover in place of a lawn.

In the Landscape

Most mosses grow best in heavily shaded areas where the soil is acidic and not well drained. Low areas beneath large trees are ideal habitats for these primitive native plants. You also can grow moss between stepping-stones, in the cracks of unmortared brick walkways, and beneath larger shrubs. While mosses are not extremely delicate plants, they cannot tolerate heavy wear. Incorporate flat stones or other hard surfaces into the most frequently traveled routes through your moss garden. Also make sure that a water supply is within convenient reach, for mosses thrive on moisture. However, once they are established, they can easily survive periods of drought. Moss makes a good companion for ferns, hostas, and other shade-loving plants.

Species and Selections

Mosses grow wild in moist places throughout the South. They are most commonly found along stream banks, near drainage ditches, and in heavily wooded areas where the soil rarely dries out completely in winter. Identifying individual species is difficult and requires a magnifying glass and good botanical knowledge of how mosses grow. But collecting mosses for your yard does not require that you know their names. Simply find a wild place that is well endowed with moss and, using a shovel or trowel, dig or lift brownie-sized squares or circles when the moss and the earth attached to it are damp. Fall and spring are the ideal times to collect mosses.

You will probably notice slight differences in the color and texture of the mosses you find, which suggests that the mosses are of several species. When planting mosses in your yard, it is best to begin with several different types. Over time, the ones that find your yard most hospitable will emerge as the dominant species.

AT A GLANCE

❖

MOSS
Numerous species

Features: velvety texture

Colors: green

Height: up to 2 inches

Light: shade

Soil: moist, acidic

Water: medium to high

Range: all Zones

Pests: none specific

Remarks: ideal for damp shade

Planting and Care

Preparing a site for moss is simple. Rake up fallen leaves and pine straw, pull out weeds and grasses, and lightly scratch open the soil with a heavy dirt rake or a pronged hoe. You may till the spot lightly, though this is not often feasible when you are working around large tree roots. Sloping areas that are prone to erosion can be amended with rocks or pebbles. Plant ferns, hostas, and other companion plants before you plant your moss. These other plants benefit from good soil preparation, but standing or working on top of newly planted moss may kill it.

Mosses are generally collected rather than purchased. Keep your pieces of moss moist until you plant them. To plant moss, push the pieces into the loosened soil and water well. If the pieces insist on popping up out of the soil, weigh them down with small stones or pebbles. You can help moss fill in quickly by inoculating the area with more moss and spores (spores are contained in the capsules found atop the plants' slender brown stalks). The easiest way to do this is to make a "moss milk shake" by taking patches of moss, putting them in a blender with buttermilk, and blending for a few seconds. Dab or scatter this mixture wherever you want new moss to grow.

Because mosses do not have true roots and essentially grow on top of the ground, they benefit more from frequent light watering than from the deep soakings preferred by other plants. And although mosses love shade, they often grow most vigorously in autumn, just after the leaves have fallen. To make sure your moss gets plenty of light during this important time, promptly rake or sweep leaves or pine straw from your moss garden. Fall is also the best time to lightly fertilize moss with liquid fertilizer diluted to half strength.

A carpet of moss is as handsome as any lawn and will thrive in the damp, shady areas where many lawn grasses struggle.

Pachysandra, Japanese

The white edges of variegated selections of pachysandra will bring a sparkle to shady beds.

The aristocrat of ground covers for shade, Japanese pachysandra (also known as Japanese spurge) has upright rosettes of leaves that cover the ground like thousands of little umbrellas. Unsurpassed when planted in broad sweeps, pachysandra is also good for covering the ground beneath azaleas, rhododendrons, or boxwoods, for it enjoys the same kind of rich, slightly acidic soil that is best for these shrubs. Pachysandra absolutely requires shade in the South, and it will grow beneath oaks where many other plants fail to thrive. Occasionally, this ground cover produces tiny fragrant flowers, but the best reason to grow pachysandra is for its lush, handsome foliage.

In the Landscape

Pachysandra's year-round color and form make it a great ground cover for planting in mass between walkways and swaths of lawn. Pachysandra spreads by developing underground rhizomes, but it is a slow spreader that rarely becomes invasive. You can use inexpensive plastic edging materials along the perimeter of the bed to stop pachysandra from sneaking into adjoining lawns or flowerbeds; within a few weeks after installing such an edging, the low, dense foliage will have completely hidden it from view.

Species and Selections

The most common form of pachysandra *(Pachysandra terminalis)*, usually sold in 2-inch pots by species name only, develops whorls of dark, olive green leaves that are about 3 inches long and have slightly toothed tips. A selection called Green Sheen is similar but has glossier, darker green leaves. The most widely available variegated pachysandra is Silver Edge. This selection grows only 6 to 8 inches tall and is slower to fill in than the green forms. However, Silver Edge has a highly refined look that makes it ideal for edging brick walkways or underplanting beneath deciduous shrubs in high-visibility beds.

There is a native American species of pachysandra called Alleghany pachysandra *(Pachysandra procumbens)* that is more clump-forming in habit and often drops its leaves in winter. While not as useful as Japanese pachysandra for a ground cover, it is a good small plant to mass in native woodland gardens.

Planting and Care

Pachysandra requires rich, fertile soil that has been improved with a 3-inch blanket of organic matter such as compost or leaf mold. Dig the bed well to mix in these soil amendments thoroughly, and add a controlled-release fertilizer. Water the prepared bed the day before planting, making sure it is completely moist. Set out well-rooted plants 6 to 12 inches apart, and mulch between them with a 2-inch layer of pine needles or finely shredded bark (soil conditioner). Water your new planting as often as needed during its first summer to help the plants fill in quickly. Because most of pachysandra's new growth develops in early summer, spring is the best time to create a new bed. In areas of the lower South where the temperature remains high at night, growth (spreading) is slower than in the cooler regions of the South.

In subsequent years, feed pachysandra twice during the summer to keep the plants vigorous and healthy. Along with the first feeding in early spring, cover the area with 1 inch of compost to help maintain the soil's organic matter content and encourage rooting as the plants spread. Fertilize a second time in late summer. Noticeable yellowing of pachysandra leaves is usually due to too much sun but also can be a sign of nutrient deficiency. If you see yellowing in the shade, apply a product that will supply iron such as Ironite.

You can propagate pachysandra by taking rooted cuttings from established plantings in late spring and transplanting them right away in rich, moist soil. Or sink the cuttings in pots and allow them to develop strong roots before moving them to a new bed. Older plantings in dense shade sometimes become leggy, but you can encourage them to become bushy by pinching off the top inch or so of the growing tips in late spring. This is best done with a pair of handheld clippers or shears, for serious shearing can badly damage the plants.

Troubleshooting

Pachysandra may develop leaf blight which turns the leaves black. Caused by a fungus, the blight is worst during wet weather, especially in beds where the planting is dense and the leaves were not raked off the plants in fall. To control leaf blight, spray with a recommended fungicide at the first sign of its presence. Also, thin crowded plantings, and be sure to rake leaves from the bed in fall.

Pachysandra forms a graceful, elegant ground cover when grown in rich soil and shade.

Periwinkle, Common

Common periwinkle is a low, colorful, easily grown ground cover.

A fast-spreading evergreen ground cover, common periwinkle is famous for its lavender blue flowers that appear each spring and its low-maintenance requirements. Also known as vinca or myrtle, periwinkle is a common ground cover used in the South because it is easy to grow and quick to cover. Once planted, periwinkle will ramble along the ground beneath azaleas, carpet craggy slopes with glossy greenery, or form puddles of blue in open woodlands when it blooms in spring.

In the Landscape

As long as it is planted in a spot that receives at least half a day of shade, periwinkle will make itself at home. This ground cover is prone to leaf burn when exposed to scorching sun; it prefers afternoon shade. Because periwinkle stays close to the ground and quickly develops new roots where the vinelike stems touch the ground, it is perfect for mass planting where you want to create an informal island of green. It also is a good ground cover for gentle slopes and makes a fine lawn alternative in small areas, provided the edges can be regularly groomed. Periwinkle cannot tolerate foot traffic, however, so stepping-stones are needed if you choose to plant this ground cover where people walk.

One of the great strengths of periwinkle is the way its texture combines with stone. When used as a ground cover near rock gardens, concrete driveways, or other hard surfaces, its meandering growth habit softens them.

Species and Selections

The traditional form of common periwinkle, often labeled with its botanical name of *Vinca minor,* has glossy, dark green leaves about 1 inch long and bears five-petaled purple flowers in spring. A selection called Alba bears white flowers, and another called Atropurpurea produces burgundy blooms. Variegata has white and green markings and is more tolerant of sun than the green-leafed types.

In the lower and coastal South, there is a similar yet larger species, *Vinca major* (greater periwinkle). The distinguishing feature between the two species is leaf size: *Vinca major* has larger leaves; *Vinca minor* has smaller leaves. *Vinca major* is better adapted to the hot, humid climate of the lower and coastal South. Also known as big leaf periwinkle, *Vinca major* spreads rapidly and develops upright stems that may reach 18 inches in height. The variegated form of *Vinca major,* Variegata is useful in shaded beds in woodland settings

---

AT A GLANCE

❖

COMMON PERIWINKLE
Vinca minor

Features: dwarf habit, lustrous leaves

Colors: purplish blue, burgundy, or white flowers

Height: 4 to 8 inches

Light: partial to full shade

Soil: well drained

Water: medium

Range: Zones 4 to 7

Pests: none specific

Remarks: top choice for shade

and often serves as a trailing accent plant in window boxes and other containers. Green-leafed *Vinca major* is a wild rambler that tends to become invasive and should be considered as a ground cover only in places where no other plants are likely to grow.

Planting and Care

In shady areas where periwinkle will not be faced with competition from sun-loving weeds, planting is a simple matter of setting plants 12 inches apart in cultivated soil so that their roots are barely covered and keeping the soil and plants damp for about two weeks. At any time of year except midwinter, you can also dig rooted pieces from established stands and transplant them to where you want them to grow. As long as the transplanted pieces have a few roots and are kept moist for a week or so after planting, they should grow well. You can also purchase transplants in 2-inch pots to set out in spring.

In spots where Bermuda or any wild grasses or weeds have grown in the past, be sure you eradicate all weeds before planting the periwinkle. Although periwinkle will grow in weedy situations, it will not look its best. When planting periwinkle in woodland or natural garden settings, many gardeners underplant this ground cover with yellow daffodils, which multiply and spread easily.

Established periwinkle needs little care beyond trimming the edges of the planting once or twice a year. In late autumn, after the leaves and pine straw have fallen, lightly rake off any leaves that have accumulated on top of the periwinkle. This will allow periwinkle's leaves to benefit from winter sunshine.

Common periwinkle covers the ground with a network of vines that root where they touch the ground.

Star Jasmine, Japanese

Very popular in the lower and coastal South, Japanese star jasmine is a vine that knits together to form a dense ground cover.

Tremendously tolerant of heat and humidity, Japanese star jasmine (also called Asian star jasmine) is a ground-hugging vine similar in appearance to common periwinkle. Yet it grows much better in the lower South than does periwinkle and can also tolerate substantially more sun. Japanese star jasmine cannot tolerate the hard winter freezes, however, so it is rarely grown north of Montgomery, Alabama, and Jackson, Mississippi.

This lush, deep green ground cover looks like its popular, fragrant cousin, Confederate jasmine. But the leaves of Japanese star jasmine are smaller and more delicate, and this vine is not as insistent about climbing up anything in its path, preferring instead to stay close to the ground. The young leaves of Japanese star jasmine are glossy bright green and turn darker green as they mature. The plant also has creamy yellow flowers that appear in spring, and though they are not particularly showy, they are intensely fragrant.

In the Landscape

Japanese star jasmine will twine up a support such as a trellis, but it is most often used as a ground cover. It spreads by winding woody stems across the surface of the ground, making it a good choice for rocky areas, banks, or wherever stumps are a problem. Another asset of this plant is its ability to prevent erosion. And since the vines are capable of forming a thick carpet up to 12 to 15 inches deep, they make a good foundation planting under low windows or porches.

This ground cover will tolerate sunny locations but fares much better in partial shade, especially when grown in areas surrounded by concrete or asphalt where heat is reflected. It is also tolerant of dense shade, making it an excellent replacement for lawn grasses that are not suitable for shady areas and a wonderful plant for carpeting the ground below live oaks and other dense trees. Since Japanese star jasmine has a vigorous growth habit in the lower South, plant it next to an edging so that you can easily trim it to help keep it looking neat. When planting Japanese star jasmine in pathways, include stepping-stones or another walking surface, for the plants cannot survive foot traffic.

Japanese star jasmine makes an attractive cover over bulb plantings. When the bulbs pop through the thick mat, they are framed by the handsome evergreen foliage. The remainder of the year the ground cover serves as a pleasant contrast to surrounding lawn or paving.

Species and Selections

Japanese star jasmine *(Trachelospermum asiaticum)* is sold in individual containers. Make sure the plants are of the correct species, for they are easily confused with Confederate jasmine *(Trachelospermum jasminoides),* which is sometimes called star jasmine (but never Japanese or Asian star jasmine). Japanese star jasmine is slightly more cold tolerant than Confederate jasmine and has a more compact growth habit.

Planting and Care

This tough, vigorous ground cover requires no special handling. Prepare the ground as you would for any ground cover, making sure any perennial weeds are removed before the plants are set in the ground. Japanese star jasmine will grow in poor soils but will do better if organic matter such as peat moss or compost is mixed into the soil to help it retain moisture during dry spells. Space plants 15 inches apart and mulch between them with pine straw or shredded bark to keep the soil moist and deter weeds. When planted in spring, the plants should fill in the spaces between them in a year.

After the plants are established, trim the perimeter of the planting two or three times during the summer to keep it in bounds. You might also fertilize the planting lightly each spring to help encourage new growth. In the event that the leaves become damaged by unusually severe winter weather, clip off the damaged stems in early spring to make the planting look neat.

Troubleshooting

Occasionally, Japanese star jasmine may become infested with scales and whiteflies, tiny insects that feed on new leaves and stems. Both can usually be controlled by promptly treating the infested plants with insecticidal soap.

Japanese star jasmine trims very neatly but will require edging several times during the growing season.

115

Wintercreeper

The upright, young stems of wintercreeper give it a windswept look.

A trailing form of the familiar euonymus shrubs often used in foundation plantings, wintercreeper is a highly adaptable ground cover in the middle and upper South. This plant adds to the landscape by covering the ground with a nearly weed-proof tangle of green. When nights become cooler in fall, the leaves turn the color of burgundy wine, holding their red color until new growth commences in spring. On the practical side, wintercreeper is useful for erosion control since the stems develop roots where they come in contact with moist soil.

In the Landscape

Wintercreeper will grow in sun or shade, though partial shade is usually best. The vinelike plants develop roots that can cling to trees and buildings, but they can easily be discouraged from climbing with regular trimming. The best uses for this ground cover are on gentle slopes and in rocky areas where the stems can wander freely. Avoid using wintercreeper alongside walkways or lawns where you want to maintain a clean edge, for the stems will continually sneak beyond their boundaries. Since wintercreeper often requires a bit more grooming than other ground covers, it is wise to plant it in a place that is easily accessible.

Wintercreeper's rich red winter colors contrast beautifully with dormant warm-season lawns and make an eye-catching accent for stone walls or other types of masonry. All of the wintercreepers are evergreen, but very severe winter weather occasionally will cause them to drop their leaves. When this happens, use the opportunity to shear back the damaged plants, and rake away the accumulated debris. In spring, new growth will appear stronger than ever.

Different Selections

The most brightly colored wintercreeper, Coloratus (sometimes called purple wintercreeper) is also famous for its vigor. The 2-inch-long leaves of Coloratus remain dark green all summer and turn burgundy red in late fall. Acutus is a similar selection with slightly smaller leaves.

Variegated wintercreepers show white leaf edges all summer; these edges turn pink in the fall and winter. Gracilis has lighter hues both summer and winter, while Emerald Gaiety becomes very dark pink by early winter. Golden Edge is known for its bright yellow-green variegated foliage. You can use cuttings from these selections for flower arrangements year-round.

AT A GLANCE
❖
WINTERCREEPER
Euonymus fortunei

Features: dramatic leaf colors

Colors: green to red

Height: 1 to 2 feet

Light: partial sun to filtered shade

Soil: rich, well drained

Water: medium

Range: Zones 6 to 8

Pests: Euonymus scale

Remarks: excellent for slopes

These large-leafed wintercreepers are the best choices as ground covers in large spaces, but so-called miniature wintercreepers, including the Kewensis selection, make lovely low carpets for small spaces or large containers planted with upright evergreen shrubs. Kewensis grows much more slowly than other wintercreepers, and its tiny $\frac{1}{2}$-inch-long leaves give the plant a very fine texture.

Golden Edge wintercreeper adds a bright touch to this bed.

Planting and Care

Wintercreeper will grow in well-drained soil; however, it grows more slowly in poor soil than it does in rich, moist soil. Plants are often sold in small 4-inch pots. If you are planting a large area, see whether your nursery can obtain less costly bare-root plants for you. Plant container-grown or bare-root plants 12 inches apart, water them well, and mulch between the plants to suppress weeds. Mulch also encourages the stems to root as they spread across the bed. When planted in spring and watered during dry spells, wintercreeper can cover a space completely in only a year or two.

In early spring, when new growth is just beginning, prune wintercreeper lightly to give the planting shape and to stimulate new growth. Go through the planting with pruning shears, cutting off damaged stems and any plant parts that show unusual leaf shapes or color. This ground cover is famous for spontaneously producing shoots that are different from the parent plants.

Troubleshooting

A tiny insect, Euonymus scale can seriously infect wintercreeper, especially in the warmest sections of the South. If you see mysterious yellowing or wilting of leaves, check for the presence of this pest, which can often be found clinging to stems and the undersides of leaves. In cool weather, you may be able to bring scale under control with a thorough application of horticultural oil spray. If the scale problem persists, use an approved insecticide for euonymus shrubs.

Diseases, Insects, and Weeds

If diseases, insects, or weeds appear in your lawn or ground cover, identify them as quickly as possible so that you can control them early.

Timing is very important when controlling diseases, insects, and weeds. Weeds grow most rapidly in spring and fall; insects and diseases are seasonal as well. The best control is to maintain the overall health of your lawn. Poor growing conditions or improper care often allows diseases, insects, and weeds to gain a foothold.

Diseases

Lawns that are maintained properly are not likely to be destroyed by an outbreak of disease. Too much or too little fertilizer, improper mowing height, and heavy thatch will encourage disease. However, if you do suspect a fungus or other disease, it is critical to identify the problem and treat the lawn immediately, as diseases spread rapidly. Some diseases are difficult to diagnose just by looking at the grass; if you have a recurring problem, send samples for analysis to an Agricultural Extension Service laboratory.

Diseases are worst in rainy weather, heavy fog, or dew because most diseases generally need moisture to thrive. For this reason, you should always water your grass very early in the morning, when it is probably already wet from dew or fog. By doing this, you will not extend the number of hours that the grass blades stay moist.

When applying fungicides, be sure to treat the entire lawn, not just the damaged area. Also, avoid mowing for a week or longer, and collect clippings when you mow.

Brown Patch

Brown patch is a very common fungal disease that can affect all types of lawn grasses. It is most likely to attack lawns that are overfertilized. Brown patch appears as circular, blighted spots when the weather is warm and humid. The spots may be only a few inches across or as wide as 3 feet. Sometimes grass at the center of the patch will begin growing again, giving the patch the appearance of a doughnut. At the first sign of this disease, stop watering and fertilizing the lawn, and bag mowed clippings to help the grass dry out quickly. If the problem worsens, use an approved fungicide to bring it under control. Take-all patch is a disease that also may appear as circular spots; it kills the grass, including the roots, and thus there is no regrowth in the center. Spray the affected area with an approved fungicide. Replant after treating.

Brown Patch

Crown Rot

Crown rot, a fungus that is worst during a period of hot, humid weather, causes some ground cover plants such as ajuga to collapse and shrivel. If this occurs, trim the infected leaves and top-dress the area with an inch of compost. If the ground cover's new growth from the old roots does not appear healthy, till or turn the soil in areas where growth is weak; add organic matter to the soil to improve drainage before replanting the ground cover. Where crown rot is a recurring problem, consider using another ground cover in the affected site, and move your healthy plants to a better-drained location.

Dollar Spot

Dollar Spot

This disease is often an indication that a lawn needs more fertilizer. It is caused by a fungus and is most common on Bahia, Bermuda, and Zoysia. Dollar spot is often worst in spring and fall, when temperatures are mild and there is heavy dew. The spots are only a few inches in diameter and are typically a light straw-brown color. To correct the problem, provide proper fertilizer and water. Persistent dollar spot may require two or three applications of an approved fungicide.

Fairy Ring

Fairy ring is a fungal disease that appears in ring-like patterns of dark green grass, dead grass, or mushrooms on the lawn. Mushrooms are likely to appear in the rings, especially in late summer and fall. This disease is most common in areas that were once wooded or in spots where tree stumps lie underground. It may also appear in lawns which have a thick layer of thatch. The fungus grows from decaying organic matter in the lawn. Damage is worst in lawns that are not fertilized. The soil in the ring may become very dry from the fungal growth and then difficult to keep wet. Competition for water or byproducts of the fungus may kill your grass.

The best way to avoid fairy ring is to water and fertilize properly to prevent thatch buildup. On new home sites, be sure that old tree stumps are thoroughly ground up and removed before planting grass.

Fairy Ring

Gray Leaf Spot

This disease attacks only St. Augustine grass, especially St. Augustine that is newly planted. The fungus causes olive green spots on the grass blades that later turn brown. A severely affected lawn will look scorched. Gray leaf spot is worst during warm, humid weather in spring and will often disappear on its own as soon as the weather gets hot.

St. Augustine Decline Virus (SADV)

St. Augustine decline virus (SADV) also only attacks St. Augustine grass. It first shows up as a faint mottling and yellowing of the grass blades. The grass then gradually fades away, leaving the area bare or weedy. The only control for SADV is to plant resistant selections such as Floralawn, Floratam, and Seville.

Snow Mold

Also called Fusarium patch, snow mold shows up in circular patches and develops under tree leaves that remain on the lawn for the winter. At first, patches are gray or light tan but may turn pink or salmon after exposure to light. This disease is worst when snow falls on unfrozen ground. Succulent growth as well as poor air circulation and soggy conditions encourage its development. Avoid snow mold by raking leaves after they fall. Also, do not fertilize before cold, wet weather or the snowy season.

Insects

Insects are a seasonal problem that may not occur every year. Below are descriptions of some of the most common insects and the signs of their presence. "Invasions" of particular insects are usually easy to recognize because they tend to occur in similar lawns throughout a region. If you suspect an insect problem, contact your county Agricultural Extension Service office for information about outbreaks in your area or the peaks in cycles of yearly pests such as mole crickets and grubs.

Chinch Bugs

Chinch bugs prefer St. Augustine grass, but they will also attack Bermuda and centipede. The tiny black-and-white bugs, which are about the size of a small grain of rice, suck sap from the grass, causing it to yellow and then turn a dry brown. Damage is usually worst during hot, dry weather and typically begins in the warmest, sunniest

Chinch Bugs

parts of the lawn. You can identify chinch bugs by looking for them at the margins of an area of yellowing grass (not where the grass is dead). If they scurry away too fast for you to identify them, try this trick: Cut off both ends of a coffee can, press the can about 1 inch into the soil, and fill it with soapy water. Any chinch bugs present will float to the top. Treat infested lawns with an insecticide labeled for chinch bugs, following label directions. Floralawn and Floratam are two selections of St. Augustine grass that are resistant to chinch bugs.

Mole Crickets

Mole crickets are the most serious pest of lawns in the lower and coastal South, but they are rarely a problem in the rest of the South. They spend most of their life tunneling through turf, eating roots as they go. Adult mole crickets, which measure about 1½ inches in length, have light brown to gray, velvety, blocky bodies and spadelike legs. You will see them come out to feed on grass stems and blades only at night, when they are attracted to lights. Damage by mole crickets is most severe in mid- to late summer, as this is when the young nymphs are feeding heavily. The best time to control these pests is in May and June, when the new generation of nymphs is young. You may also use baits or pesticides in early spring or late summer, but these will not be as effective against the larger, older insects.

Mole Cricket

Nematodes

Nematodes are microscopic, wormlike pests that live in the soil and become parasites on plant roots. They are common in the sandy soils of the Gulf South. When plants are infected, they cannot take up water and nutrients efficiently, and growth tends to be slow and weak. The types of nematodes that can weaken lawns include several species that do not cause noticeable knots or galls to form on the roots, as occurs from attacks by the well-known root knot nematode. To confirm the presence of damaging nematodes in a failing lawn, contact your county Agricultural Extension Service office for information on submitting a soil sample for analysis.

There is little you can do to kill the nematodes present, but you can care for your lawn properly as recommended in this book to be sure it grows as vigorously as possible. Because nematodes are worse in poor, sandy soil, try spreading a 1- to 2-inch layer of compost over your lawn each spring. If you should plant the lawn anew, be sure to work plenty of organic matter into the soil before planting.

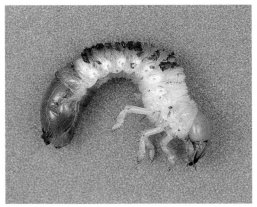

White Grub

White Grubs

The white, curled, wormlike grubs that you often encounter when digging any soil are white grubs. These grubs may be the larvae of a number of beetles, including Japanese beetles and June beetles. White grubs, and almost all lawns host some white grubs, feed on grass roots but do minimal damage if present in small numbers. However, very heavy grub feeding can injure a lawn. If the grubs are Japanese beetle larvae, they will later harm other landscape plants as well. Pesticides that are not toxic to earthworms and other beneficial insects have been developed; they successfully control grubs when applied to the soil in mid- to late spring, when the grubs are near the surface. Treat infested lawns carefully, following label directions.

Weeds

Many techniques and herbicides, or weedkillers, are available to help you manage weeds in your lawn, but the recommendations for specific products change yearly. For the names of current products, contact your county Agricultural Extension Service office, which is listed under the county governments section in the blue pages of your telephone book.

Always use weedkillers carefully, and follow label directions exactly. Any product you buy to use on lawns will list the specific lawn grasses tolerant of the weedkiller, as well as any grasses on which it should not be used. Herbicides used to control lawn weeds may injure ground covers, flowers, shrubs, or trees, so pay close attention to the direction of the wind if you are spraying. Spread granular products only on the lawn, being certain to keep them away from the roots of ornamental plants. (See page 35 for more information about the different types of weedkillers.)

Weeds fall into two categories: annual and perennial. Annual weeds, such as crabgrass and henbit, come up from seed each year. Perennial weeds, such as plantains, return from their roots. Some weeds, such as dandelions, return from their roots as well as spread by seed.

Annual Bluegrass

Annual bluegrass is one of the most common and troublesome weeds in Southern lawns. As the name implies, this black sheep of the bluegrass family is an annual, but it reseeds easily and will recur year after year if not controlled. Annual bluegrass seeds start to germinate

Flower stalk of annual bluegrass

in late summer and early fall, and the plants begin to flower and produce seeds by midwinter. This weed often mars the color and texture of dormant warm-season lawns with its tiny clumps of green and its short flower spikes. In fescue lawns, the seedheads create white patches. Some pre-emergence herbicides prevent annual bluegrass seedlings from germinating; look for a product that lists annual bluegrass as one of the weeds it controls. Apply in late summer or early fall, just before night temperatures fall below 70 degrees and new annual bluegrass seedlings come to life.

Common Chickweed

Common Chickweed

This annual weed germinates in the fall and grows quickly in cool weather to form a dark green, spreading mat. Small white flowers produce seeds that are easily carried by birds and by the wind. Chickweed is common in lawns, flowerbeds, and vegetable gardens during the winter months. Abundant chickweed in the lawn often indicates that your lawn has thinned out from too much shade or improper care. A thick, vigorous lawn will crowd out chickweed. Pull scattered individual plants by hand, spot-treat them with an herbicide spray approved for use on your lawn grass, or use a fertilizer and weed-killer combination in spring or early fall.

Crabgrass

It takes only a few crabgrass plants to give a lawn a coarse, unkempt look. Crabgrass plants grow from seeds that sprout in early spring. You can dig out the young plants, if you have only scattered plants in a lawn of Bermuda or another grass that will quickly cover the spot with new runners. However, in a tall fescue lawn or any lawn in which crabgrass is a recurrent problem, the most effective control is to use a pre-emergence herbicide in early spring, about two weeks before the last frost. Many pre-emergence controls are actually called "crabgrass preventers."

Crabgrass

Curly Dock

Curly dock, a perennial weed that prefers moist, heavy soil, develops an extensive taproot. Any piece of the root remaining in the soil will grow a new plant. In addition, greenish flower stalks appearing in summer drop seeds that sprout in spring or fall. Eliminate plants by spot-treating with an herbicide spray approved for use on your type of lawn grass. You may need to apply again if the weed sprouts a

Curly Dock

Dandelion

Henbit

Plantain

second time. After you eliminate existing curly dock, you can prevent future problems by fertilizing your lawn properly and mowing it 2 inches or higher.

Dandelion

A widespread weed in lawns, dandelion blooms from spring through fall and also in winter during mild spells. The fluffy plumes attached to its seeds help the seeds float for miles. Seeds may germinate in spring or fall. Like curly dock, dandelion grows a taproot that is difficult to pull up in one piece. However, you can pry out young plants with a handtool known as a dandelion weeder or a fishtail weeder. Thick grass cut at the proper height will keep dandelion seeds from germinating. Treat large outbreaks in spring with an herbicide spray approved for use on your type of lawn grass.

Henbit

Despite its pretty lavender flowers, this winter annual can be a persistent pest. It germinates in fall and winter, forms dark green clumps by spring, and then drops its seed and dies as the weather turns warm. Henbit is an opportunist, sprouting in spots where grass has thinned or died. It is common in warm-season lawns that have turned brown for the winter. Keep the lawn vigorous through proper fertilization, watering, and mowing at the proper height to discourage henbit. Pull scattered henbit by hand. Spot-treat more seriously affected areas with a liquid herbicide or a fertilizer and weedkiller combination recommended for use on your type of lawn grass.

Plantain

Plantains are perennial broadleaf weeds that often appear in damp, compacted soils, especially in shade. They spread by seeds, with new seedlings usually appearing in the spring. There are two types of plantains, buckhorn and broadleaf. Buckhorn plantain has thin, straplike leaves, while broadleaf plantain has leaves three to four times as wide.

Control plantains with a recommended broadleaf weedkiller. To prevent future problems, you will need to aerate your lawn and plant a shade-tolerant grass that can compete with the weed.

White Clover

Present in all types of lawns, white clover is both a blessing and a curse. Clover produces flowers that attract honeybees and other beneficial insects, but clover's texture is different from that of lawn grasses. You can often control white clover by carefully managing your lawn grass. Increase the frequency of fertilizer applications, and mow high and often to promote strong grass growth. In situations in which the clover is well established and is growing so thickly that it is shading the grass extensively, control white clover by using a broadleaf weedkiller approved for use on your grass. As with any post-emergence weedkiller, use only when the plant is actively growing.

Wild Onion and Wild Garlic

Similar in appearance, these two onionlike perennial weeds are among the hardest to control. They reproduce rapidly by underground bulblets and aboveground bulbils and seed. Often sprouting in late fall and winter, they are very conspicuous in warm-season lawns that have turned brown for the winter. Eradicate clumps of wild onion and wild garlic as they appear, in order to remove the source of bulblets, bulbils, and seed. If you have only a few clumps, dig them by hand, being sure to pull up all of the bulbs. The sooner you remove these weeds the better, as large, older plants are harder to get rid of. To control numerous clumps, spot-treat them in winter or spring with a liquid weedkiller recommended for use on your type of lawn grass. Because herbicides work slowly in cold weather, several applications may be necessary. It helps to crush the plants underfoot as this will scrape away some of the waxy coating that protects them from weedkillers.

White Clover

Wild Onion and Wild Garlic

Index

Index

Special Thanks

Jim Bathie, photographs 60, 85
Arlyn W. Evans, photographs 122
Derek Fell, photographs 31, 65, 68, 71,
    86, 87, 91, 116, 117
Barbara Pleasant, photographs 90, 112
University of Florida Institute of Food and
    Agricultural Sciences (http://gnv.ifas.ufl.edu),
    photograph 120
Cathy Ritter
Southern Progress Corporation Library Staff